Your Vegan Story

The Why and How People Become Vegan

RAMINTA GRIGAITĖ

ISBN: 979-8-849207-59-9

DEDICATION

I dedicate this book to those about to embark on their vegan journey so they can later tell their vegan story.

Let's connect

https://www.instagram.com/yourveganstory_/

https://twitter.com/yourveganstory

https://www.tiktok.com/@yourveganstory

Share your story: **#MyVeganStory**
Share the quote: **#VeganStoryQuote**

Dear Del!
I hope you will enjoy reading this book and you'll find something that will make you smile!
The future is vegan. Congratulations for being at the forefront!

Raminta x

Contents

ACKNOWLEDGMENTS

First, I must thank all the vegans whose incredible stories birthed this book. Thank you to anyone who shared and keeps on sharing their vegan story, extends their hand to help a starting vegan, and is willing to give advice and encouragement to those who seek it. Your words empower, encourage, and give hope for a better future. Keep being kind and emphatic. Thank you because this book would not be possible without you and your vegan stories.

Most of what I understand about veganism came from other people, from devoted animal rights activists and those who are passionate about being truly healthy, both physically and emotionally. I thank these people for their continuous dedication to improving the world.

INTRODUCTION

Every author, I suppose, embarking on such a challenge as writing a book would like the readers to enjoy it and gain a perspective and benefit from having read it. I hope to enrich your understanding of why people choose to go vegan and delve deeper into how they do it. Why care about these questions at all? We, humans, are curious creatures, and other people's stories are especially intriguing to us. They help relate to each other, learn good/bad behaviours, and give a sense of belonging to a social group, providing connectedness to a community. The need to belong is one of the key emotional needs and leads to a more fulfilling life.

While writing this book, it was particularly challenging to identify the reader. I genuinely believe that those who are already vegan and the biggest veganism sceptics would benefit equally and find something valuable for themselves. If you are the former, I hope it will inspire you to further spread the word about veganism. Feel free to gift this book once finished to the one person you had in mind while reading. And if you are the latter, I hope you will continue reading with an open heart and mind. I firmly believe this book will work for those who are yet to try veganism to gain inspiration, motivation, and a sense of community. For current vegans it will provide a sense of belonging to a vast group of people who, just like them, chose a vegan lifestyle and have many relatable stories. Quite notably, this book will serve as a resource for those in activism by providing perspective and understanding of how and why people become vegan. It will help activists relate better and communicate more effectively to those willing to change or open to listening with a heart.

Most important disclaimer is that I do not aim to convince anyone to go vegan simply because I cannot. The power is in each individual's hands. My role here is to share the vegan stories.

In this book, I will aim to answer the questions of why and how people go vegan. By answering them in a structured way, primarily through personal experiences, I aim to touch the heart of vegans and non-vegans alike. Firstly, for vegans, it would tell the perspective of others and see their own experiences reflected in someone else's story. You may nod or smile at these pages, recognizing similar feelings you had on your journey to veganism. Secondly, this book will offer a great perspective to non-vegans. If you are one of them and would like to start your own vegan journey, we are waiting for you in our welcoming vegan communities across the globe. I invite you to share your vegan story with a #MyVeganStory so that we all can support you and learn from your account. In the coming chapters, you will find different reasons why someone is vegan and how eventually those reasons intertwine, creating a situation where everybody wins. You will also find the multiple ways how someone becomes vegan, from going cold turkey to making a gradual shift, being vegetarian for decades, or being influenced by the family member and their changing habits.

In my humble opinion, this book will offer an excellent understanding for the families and friends of those vegans who seek support from their close ones. So, if you are vegan and your immediate circle is not, make sure you let your loved ones read this book and feel it through. Let me know by contacting @myveganstory on social media or posting #MyVeganStory if sharing this book enabled you to connect better with your acquaintances. I hope it will help you build a stronger relationship, rather than getting further apart due to the changes in the lifestyle and the lack of mutual understanding resulting from it. I would appreciate you sharing your story. Connecting with the real people who have been positively impacted will make an effort count the most!

Anyone who considers themselves vegan can attest that they've heard the following question from someone with a surprised expression: why did you become vegan? In the coming pages, you will read a compilation of thoroughly selected, reviewed, and assembled individual experiences of why and how a person went vegan. These stories were carefully sourced from openly shared comments across social media. Without people who passionately tell their stories, give advice, and support newbies, there would be fewer vegans and much more suffering worldwide. Only through positive association we as humanity can move forward to the vegan future quicker.

Therefore, I wrote this book, editing and systematising your shared stories so that they would be heard by more people helping them to take the necessary step toward a better future.

1 STORIES. WHY DO THEY MATTER?

You're never going to kill storytelling because it's built into the human plan. We come with it.
Margaret Atwood

As the title implies, this book is about stories. Stories about becoming vegan, the why and the how, including the good, the bad, and the ugly. They are beautifully unique yet similar, stemming from a common empathy root for the non-human animals, your health, or our planet.

I hope that any vegan reading this book can relate and verbalise the feelings that sometimes are difficult to express. You may find fragments of yourself and sympathetically nod at the pages. We often find ourselves in other people's words, seeing the same picture from a different perspective and thus understanding ourselves and our feelings better. And if you are reading the book from the standpoint of a non-vegan, I hope these stories from real people will help you better understand why people go vegan, what inspires them, and how they do it.

Since through stories we get to know and understand people better, perhaps this book will help you relate more to your close friend, children, or siblings. Who knows, maybe you have been gifted this book by someone who would appreciate a bit more understanding from you. Having more context from the stories of many people with different backgrounds and ages will lead you in the right direction to have meaningful conversations with your acquaintance if you wish to relate more. And I'm guessing you are already on the same page about not wanting to hurt animals. This book will take this meaning to another level.

Some stories tell us why people go vegan, what made them choose this lifestyle, what was the most difficult, what was the easiest part, and what vegans miss the most. I hope you can better connect emotionally with why people choose to go vegan and perhaps, if not choosing it for yourself, better understand and support important people in your life.

STORYTELLING

Before the books and the written word were invented, storytelling was all those humans had, yet in the abundance of ways to communicate, it is still the best form of information transmission. Storytelling is universal across time and cultures and recorded history, from Mesopotamia to small villages in rural islands. Simply, it is easier for our brain to understand the meaning and assimilate the knowledge if it is told through stories.

You might wonder, isn't sharing facts and statistics about veganism enough to help people see for themselves what it is all about? Indeed, facts and information alone can convince people, but they don't inspire. Stories, on the other hand, are so powerful in eliciting emotions, connection, and igniting motivation. They can shape beliefs and change minds. Due to our social roots, we humans are hardwired to share stories. We enjoy sharing personal anecdotes as much as we love listening to other people's experiences. This way, we feel part of the social group, fulfilling our basic need for connection. Storytelling is a powerful medium through which our everyday emotions and memories flow and interconnect. Even modern neurological researchers agree that storytelling is the best way to capture attention creating deeper personal bonds between the storytellers and listeners.

Listening or reading stories activates our mirror neurons. We can feel sympathy or agreement, mirroring others' brain activity. Being social creatures, we strive to feel connected through shared emotions and stories. In fact, as a species, we are addicted to stories. Hence media is profiting off of this. Unfortunately, primarily negative stories and scandalous news attract our attention the most. Instead, I'm hoping to inspire, ignite passion and paint a hopeful, brighter image for the future. The positive change is coming.

What questions will the stories in this book help us answer the best? There are six key questions; who, what, when, where, why, and how. They help us interrogate each situation and understand it from all angles. Although here, with the help of personal stories written by fellow vegans, I will attempt to answer the why and how of veganism.

THE STORIES

In the following pages, you will find the stories collected from over a hundred and fifty people who have decided to live life on the veg. Some of them are lengthier, while others only have the name of the seminar or documentary that people watched, influencing them to go vegan overnight without ever looking back.

The stories presented in this book were collected from English and Lithuanian speakers. Therefore, some texts were translated into the English language. Many others were edited to give a bit of context and remove any unnecessary/personal information while still keeping it authentic. What I found is that no matter the language or part of the world the stories are coming from, you are capable of relating and connecting to them. Vegans are all passionate about the same thing – to make the world a better and kinder place, bring more peace to every kind. Each vegan story tells about a unique path that was taken or the most influencing reasons leading to change a life for the better; better self, better for the animals and the planet.

The texts that you will find presented here were carefully selected, anonymised, translated, grouped, and organised into chapters. It was initially daunting to find a way to represent them all in a structured and cohesive manner, but dividing the book into two main parts of how and why with subdivided chapters was the winning option. Still, regardless of how much I tried to categorise the stories, many reasons for choosing a vegan lifestyle intertwine, which I will discuss in part "WHY". Likewise, there are many approaches to transitioning to veganism from cold turkey to years of growing understanding about veganism until something in your head finally clicks. Again, this will be discussed further in part "HOW". These two questions will be the main ones to be unravelled in the chapters ahead.

Going through forums and comments, I have seen many people were curious about how and why people go vegan, and the answers fascinated me. So, the idea was born to collect and compile all (or the rigorously selected few) the answers so that experience and wisdom can go beyond the online world and ignite compassion in more people's lives. I wholeheartedly thank people who share their genuine insights and guidance for newbies.

I will start by stepping back from the stories and dive into statistics. Then, in the next chapter, I will discuss the general veganism trends and your stories as a collection.

2 THE NUMBERS

Everything that can be counted does not necessarily count; everything that counts cannot necessarily be counted.
Albert Einstein

While stories help us relate at the individual level, numbers allow us to better understand the world surrounding us, giving it a quantifiable perspective. Although some static numbers usually may not do much in painting the whole picture thus, let me share with you some current trends surrounding veganism and what I have observed and quantified from your vegan stories.

Before we jump into the numbers and trends, let's define what the word vegan encompasses. If you have been vegan for a while, you've likely had to use the following phrases; yes, chicken is meat; no, fish isn't vegan; no, I don't consume dairy. What it shows is the lack of definition and understanding in the broader population of what really those mysterious vegans eat. But if you, the curios soul, are not vegan and have been gifted this book by a caring relative or spouse or are deeply intrigued, what it means to be a vegan and how it is defined, I will help you understand.

Oxford dictionary describes a vegan as a "person who does not eat any food derived from animals and who typically does not use other animal products". The more comprehensive definition comes from the Vegan Society: "to seek an end to the use of animals by man for food, commodities, work, hunting, vivisection, and by all other uses involving exploitation of animal life by man".

This will be the definition I am sticking with to be on the same page about what vegan means throughout the book.

PLANT-BASED IS ON THE RISE

Perhaps it is unnecessary to explain that veganism is rising, as it is evident when you stand in the milk aisle at the supermarket. The overwhelming number of available options of various plant milk is slowly pushing out the dairy milk and taking the dominance. Even the fussiest person can find what suits them best in their cuppa. Different plants have been milked, ranging from peas and potatoes to cashew nuts and hemp seeds. Almond milk is the most popular drink in the US, while in UK's first place is taken by oat milk, the latter being friendlier to the environment too.

Dairy milk alternatives are just one example of expanding plant-based food options. Anything you could think of, a vegan version has been produced at greater or lesser success. I am incredibly excited about the future and what new tastes it will bring us, the advanced vegans and the newbies alike. In fact, not only are new food items available in the stores, but even the big chains are continuously bringing out some of the most loved products to the market. Mcdonald's McPlant™ is one of the success stories. Having these options at known establishments helps meat-eaters to try them out, and flexitarians/vegans enjoy it while out with a group. There were multiple examples recently of the big fast-food chains introducing superior options for a plant-based customer. One of the Burger King branches at Liverpool Street station at the heart of London transformed the store into a fully meat-free for one month. KFC has introduced Beyond Fried Chicken, seeing the potential in the ever-growing niche of meat alternatives. Of course, you could argue that these brands exploit animals *en masse*, and supporting them with your pocket is hypocritical. Still, I firmly believe it is for the best in the long run, as it normalises the plant-based alternatives for a much broader population.

When it comes to satisfying a sweet tooth, big brands have created their own vegan versions of the most popular chocolate bars. Numerous independent chocolateries are also creating sweets out of this world and vegan bakeries surprise the most prominent food connoisseurs. Thanks to the easily whippable double cream and creative recipes, the vegan cakes look good and taste guilt-free. When I say guilt-free, I am not referring to the calories, but the fact that no mother had to be exploited for the dairy in the making of these desserts. As of writing this, I am about to pick the recipe for our very own vegan wedding cake. I have no doubt it will be delicious and beautiful, but I am most excited to see the guests enjoy a fantastic cake without any use of eggs or dairy. If you are a bit curious, check my Instagram @yourveganstory_, I will be sharing it there!

These plant food creations demonstrate that we've come a long way since the days of vegans surviving on beans and rice while for a birthday cake enjoying a slice of watermelon. Thanks to creative entrepreneurs and retail giants, switching to a vegan lifestyle is becoming effortless. So how are we doing in making the switch?

VEGANISM TRENDS

I have rounded up some of the most important trends in veganism, so let's dig in. First, I want to acknowledge that it is inevitable for the market of plant-based food and other products to keep on growing if we want to continue existing on this planet. One of the key drivers are millennials, and Gen-Z generations, who are more conscious about sustainability and the environment, and thus are more inclined towards plant-based options for food and beyond. Additionally, critical investments are attracted to the market with a continuously growing interest, and thus the spread and depth of the reach of vegan brands is increasing. Seeing the potential, companies are investing their R&D budgets in plant-based options, leading to new product launches and further consumer interest. Yet, we do not necessarily need an increasing number of unique plant-based food offers but a growing vegan community. So, let's see if the two correlate.

One important measure to track the proportion of veganism is the sign-ups to prevalent challenges such as Veganuary. There was a continuous increase of the people willing to challenge themselves and open up for a new palette of tastes and textures for January. Over half a million people (582,538 by the end of January) have signed up for Veganuary 2021, of which 125,000 were based in the UK alone. To put this in perspective, in 2015, only 1,280 people signed up, almost a four-hundred-time difference. Nearly half, 40% of the participants are willing to continue with the vegan lifestyle [1]. 2022 has been another record-breaking year, with a slight rise in the sing-ups, reaching 600,000 participants [2]. However, I must mention that these numbers are only official sign-up rates and the estimated numbers of people taking part are up to ten times higher. Continuous R&D by entrepreneurs and new product launches are booming around January, making it more exciting and more accessible for new people to switch their food and other products to plant-based.

The Happy Cow, the blog and an app to make it easier for you to find a vegan restaurant or vegan options, has reported the growing number of listings of vegan dining places in the European capitals. They grew event through the hurdles of the pandemic on the hospitality businesses in the recent years. Interestingly, the cities are seeing a drop in vegetarian places while vegan ones are increasing, and the gap between the two continues to widen. In Europe alone, there were 3400 vegan restaurants listed by early 2022 [3]. Imagine you went to one each day; you would require over nine years of eating out every day to visit each one of them. For reference, in 2019, there were only 2600 vegan restaurants listed; thus, at this pace, the options are inexhaustible.

Food is only a fraction of veganism; thus, on their website, The Vegan Society (https://www.vegansociety.com/news/media/statistics) reports statistics relating to fashion & textiles, beauty & household, environment, health, and more. Here I will share a few key findings, but please refer to the website for the complete overview.

Fashion has also seen an increase in the demand and production of vegan alternatives. Vogue reported a rise of vegan products by 258% in the UK and US. There is a lot of space for creativity in the industry, with reports of pineapple leather, mushroom leather, cactus leather, repurposed rice husk, and recycled apple peel fibres, you name it! Of course, the usual materials, nylon, and polyester gets recycled in creative ways too. Top brands in the industry are choosing vegan fabrics and launching vegan versions of their best-selling products, such as Stan Smith Adidas sneakers.

When it comes to the beauty industry, they have their fair share of animal exploitation. Ranging from the animal testing pre-launch to the animal-derived ingredients in the product. Many (36%) of the non-meat eaters are unaware of the latter. Thankfully, this sector is the fastest to move towards veganism, with 82% of new vegan product launches in the UK being in the beauty category. Consumers are also showing an interest as for the majority of them, 77%, the label "not tested on animals" was an essential decisive factor when buying a household item.

The trend for vegan products in all categories is clear, and it is expected to keep rising, not only due to the increased demand but as a solution to move towards a sustainable world.

STATS OF YOUR VEGAN STORY

Under no circumstances this collection of vegan stories is an unbiased sample, representing the population of the world's vegans. Although many different nationalities, occupations, and ages are represented, it only scratches the surface of the diversity of the vegans out there, from world-class athletes to celebrities and political figures. As of writing this chapter, it is estimated that there are approximately 79 million vegans worldwide; thus, the story of a mere 0.0000019% is being shared here.

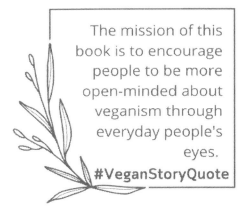

The mission of this book is to encourage people to be more open-minded about veganism through everyday people's eyes.

#VeganStoryQuote

The mission of this book is to encourage people to be more open-minded about veganism through everyday people's eyes. It illustrates different walks of life and how one stumbles upon the idea of removing animal products from their lives as far as practically possible. When switching to veganism, what seems fascinating is how things look obvious and ordinary through this newly found perspective compared to what was considered normal before. It may be frustrating and difficult to relate to anyone who hasn't chosen the vegan path yet. However, as vegans, we must be compassionate towards fellow humans, as many of us came precisely from where the most prominent opponents of veganism currently are.

Part I of the book explores the reason why behind becoming vegan. Although it is often more than just one exclusive reason, I have classified the stories to accurately represent the primary reason why. The majority, 73%, said it was for the animals, 20% for their own health, and 7% because their family member chose this lifestyle. The latter point illustrates how influential your choice to go vegan could be on your loved ones. It is common for a family member to make a switch alongside, if not complete, then partial. From my experience, my close family has shifted to drinking oat milk and ditching dairy in their coffee and morning oats. They prefer it to regular milk as a creamier alternative with a better aftertaste. So be loud and proud of sharing about your vegan journey as it could help save many lives and add more life to people.

In part II, the question of how people became vegan will be addressed, sharing examples and stories of when the switch happened and what were the most optimal ways to make the switch. People were equally happy to go cold turkey (49%) or gradually switch to veganism (51%), often coming from a vegetarian background. In fact, the average time that someone was vegetarian before switching to veganism was about 15.8 years. Many did not realise the horrors of the dairy and egg industries or their impact on personal health before becoming vegan. Often vegetarians started this way of life from a very young age or were brought up in a vegetarian family, which was an everyday reality for them.

This gives you a little glimpse of what to expect in the coming parts of WHY and HOW one becomes vegan.

PART I WHY

Find your why, and you'll find your way.
John C. Maxwell

Why is a powerful question to ask yourself, making us think deeper and connect emotionally to the actual reason behind our actions. Why is a why important? First, you need to understand why you chose a vegan lifestyle as it helps stay committed, provoking an emotional attachment to your actions. If you wish to change something important in your life, like an old habit, you need to have a clear reason behind your actions. Otherwise, the excitement soon disappears, and keeping up with your new resolutions becomes too challenging. Our brain is lazy and uses any opportunity to switch back to the old ways. You might have noticed this when you start a new routine of jogging three times a week. However, any little excuse like "it's rainy" or "I had a tiring day at work" crawls up in your head, preventing you from keeping up with those promises. If you define a solid why it helps you keep yourself accountable and disciplined about your decisions.

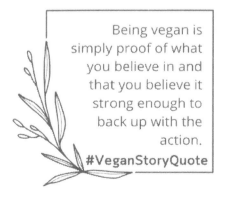

Being vegan is simply proof of what you believe in and that you believe it strong enough to back up with the action.
#VeganStoryQuote

Switching your lifestyle to a vegan one requires a lot of willpower and determination. It is particularly challenging if you embark on this journey alone and your family or friends are not only unsupportive but also keep making silly jokes. Many times, this is the case. Anywhere you go, you will see sneaky marketing of cheese and ice creams with dairy, you will be invited to BBQs and thanksgiving dinners, and work lunches will lack

15

any vegan options. Thus, shifting your mindset and heartset to veganism requires determination and self-discipline, and knowing your why will help immensely as, without it, the enthusiasm may fade away soon. Being vegan is simply proof of what you believe in and that you believe it strong enough to back up with the action.

The author Simon Sinek in his book "Start With Why" and a famous TED Talk has shared that people would only truly believe in the idea or a movement if they understood its why. Knowing and understanding your why calls for your limbic brain to be engaged which is responsible for feelings and decision-making. You may need to go deeper to unravel the more profound meaning behind your original way. Imagine peeling an onion layer to go to the core of your values and beliefs and making a solid connection with a purpose. Simply ask why for five consecutive times to dig deeper inside, to activate your superpowers. Here's an example:

Why am I vegan? I love animals too much. Why? They give me joy and awe when I see them. Why? They are incredible creatures, sharing this planet among us humans, and I'm merely a tiny part of the planet. Why? It is not up to me to take part, directly or through my money, in the mass breeding, exploitation, and killing of such creatures. And so on…

Fully understanding your why helps to keep with the commitment and stay passionate about the cause because you know exactly why you do it, and no sceptic or outside influence can change that. It is like the fuel that keeps your rocket of dedication and commitment going. It allows you to be true to yourself, align with your inner values, and act accordingly. Life becomes more peaceful with less decision fatigue.

TWO MAIN REASONS

Let's have a look into why people choose veganism. There are multiple arguments why going vegan makes sense. First, you stop indirectly participating in the mass murder of the animals in our seas and behind the walls of the slaughterhouses. It could be a wise decision from an economic standpoint as many staples such as legumes, tofu, rice, and frozen veggies are cheaper than meat or cheese. Being vegan also aligns with our inner morals of wanting to be kind and good people. It also means that eliminating animal exploitation could avoid future pandemics and epidemics of zoonotic diseases. In the past several years everyone lived through COVID-19, caused by a SARS-CoV-2. Thus, I don't need to go into further details how devastating zoonotic viruses could be financially, emotionally, and health wise. Finally, it could help solve the world's hunger problems. If we shifted to veganism and wouldn't breed billions of animals into existence to serve as intermediary for the grown food, producing calories most efficiently, going directly to consumers. The best part is that there is no sacrifice to get the above benefits. The first step is choosing to eat the rainbow instead of someone's flesh.

There are only two main reasons why people initially go vegan: for the animals and personal health. I say initially because going forward, whatever the original reason, it gets intertwined with all the other causes. Before you start being outraged, I will clarify that veganism is not a diet, and vegan food could be far from healthy. Nevertheless, many people stumble upon veganism by looking at the ways to improve their health or fight chronic illnesses. Still, upon joining the vegan community and watching some excellent documentaries, the shift in the thinking toward animals happens. Those who initially found veganism because of a healthy plant-based diet often become notorious animal's rights activists.

Let's take a closer look at what it means to be vegan for the animals.

3 VEGAN FOR THE ANIMALS

There is no fundamental difference between man and animals in their ability to feel pleasure and pain, happiness, and misery.
Charles Darwin

WE LOVE ANIMALS

If you ask a random person, there is a good chance that they will tell you they love animals. We love our animals so much that we eat meals together, take them to the parks and family trips, cuddle and play fetch with them, worry when they are sick, give them treats, brush their teeth, and ensure they have somewhere to play and their bellies are full. We even have voice-enabled video cameras for when we are stuck at work or out in town to check up on them. People love animals. In return, the animals bring us joy, happiness, loyalty, and sweet cuddles. They greet us cheerfully when we get home and come up to us when we feel sad or lonely. We go for walks and exercise together. Somehow hairs all over the apartment, poop, and other worries are unimportant because we truly love our animals. Unfortunately, when we talk about the love for animals, there are only a tiny number of species this refers to, namely cats, dogs, and perhaps an odd rabbit or a parrot.

TRUE LOVE

To truly and honestly say "I love animals" means you love them all, including the cute pink piglet and a cow with big beautiful eyes. To truly love them, we must let them be, stop breeding them by billions to the miserable life they live on a factory farm. To truly love them and to enjoy their flesh at the same time is self-deception. To truly love them while at the same time paying for someone to kill their babies is insanity. To truly love them but turn a blind eye to the apparent suffering behind the slaughterhouse is a sign of weakness. To love animals, but have a little baby, a lamb as a prominent tradition of a festivity where we are meant to celebrate the rebirth of light, life, and creation is a definition of hypocrisy.

Vegans choose to truly love animals and live without inner conflict. In fact, of those who chose veganism, the vast majority made this change to stop participating in the system where harming, abusing, and killing the animals is normalised as a primary reason. While consideration for health, ecology, the planet, and other causes come as secondary.

Although being vegan for the animals is not always straightforward and obvious. Many years of indoctrination leave us unable to make a connection between the love for animals and our own dinner plate. Shamefully, as children, we may not even know that what we ate was an animal we would otherwise choose to cuddle, laugh and run about with. Growing up, we understood that the meat on our table comes from a farm and that a steak once was a cow. However, we choose to ignore or not pay any attention to the truth. We smile at the little lambs in the fields around easter, we look in awe at the little chicks or ducklings by the river, we pet the passing dog, and if lucky enough, we look with amazement at the majestic elephants and lions in their natural habitats.

> Shamefully, as children, we may not even know that what we ate was an animal we would otherwise choose to cuddle, laugh and run about with.
>
> #VeganStoryQuote

Humans inherently love animals, yet rarely make a connection that what is on a dinner plate was once a living, laughing creature that had friends and family. The marketing in the farming industry is exceptionally potent to disguise the reality, leaving us in a comfortable blind spot, thinking that food comes from a happy, sunny place where the fields are always green and a loving farmer is petting their cow.

Another reason the connection between the steak and a sentient animal is challenging is that farm animals are typically not considered intelligent and sentient beings, but rather a number on a farm. Our perceptions, culture, and upbringing matter. This is precisely why most westerners are outraged by the dog meat festival but are comfortable with the pork on their own table.

THE INTELLIGENT ANIMALS

I will not be writing about humans, but here are some facts backed up by research evidence about common farm animals that will likely surprise you. In the upcoming sections, cognition will be defined as the mechanisms by which an individual acquires, processes, stores, and acts upon the information. It includes learning, memory, and decision-making. Intelligence is defined in many ways: the capacity for abstraction, logic, understanding, self-awareness, learning, emotional knowledge, reasoning, planning, creativity, critical thinking, and problem-solving, together with the quality of the above abilities.

Countless empirical evidence shows farmed animals possess complex emotional, cognitive, and social behavior. However, due to the bias in society, the knowledge that farm animals are intelligent is not readily accepted. Especially when comparing the intelligence and cognition of our pets, namely cats and dogs, and the animals regarded as commodities. People generally make more positive value judgments regarding animals that show cognitive similarities to humans. Let me share some of the most exciting research about four common farm animals: chickens, pigs, cattle, and sheep.

CHICKENS

According to the Food and Agriculture of the United Nations Statistical Database, in 2020, there were 37,232,972,000 chickens consumed (this number sadly includes all the ones that have been "prepared", but wasted to a landfill; however, it is a topic for another book), and they are one of the most consumed land animals. That is thirty-seven billion chickens, a number 4.7 times higher than the entire human population. This is the number of individuals killed for consumption by humans, and it is simply beyond our ability to comprehend such a vast number.

Birds are generally perceived as less intelligent and incapable of complex brain functions compared to mammals. However, studies now conclude that the distinction is not so clear, and the capacity is similar in the avian and mammalian species [4]. The intelligence of chickens is well recognized by the published, peer-reviewed scientific literature examining cognition, emotions, personality, and sociality. For example, chickens understand object permanence, recognizing that something is still present even if out of sight and can retrieve an entirely hidden object. Interestingly, chickens perform better when stimuli in the studies resemble a natural social situation. In comparison, human babies develop this ability by the age of two years.

In the math department, five-day-old chicks could perform arithmetic operations and differentiate objects containing different quantities. Rugani and co-authors did an experiment where they showed that chickens associate a smaller number with the left and a higher number with the right side (going from one to nine from left to right increasingly) [5]. They map numbers in the geometrical space similarly to many other species, including humans. Hens can also perceive time, one of the critical prerequisites to mentally represent the past and anticipate the future. In experiments, hens could self-control and delay gratification for a larger remote reward rather than a smaller proximate reward. The investigation to demonstrate this included the reward of food access for a shorter or longer time. For a two-second delay, chickens could access food for three seconds, or for a six-second delay, 22-second access was granted. Demonstrating the ability to delay gratification, chickens were able to choose the latter [6]. This is similar to the famous Stanford marshmallow experiment study with toddlers, where a child could choose between one small reward or two small rewards if they waited for the examiner to return without eating the first marshmallow [7]. For a daily dose of cuteness, it is worth searching for some videos of replication of this experiment if you have not seen it yet!

Chickens can communicate through 24 different vocalizations complemented by different visual displays. They use it to convey information and not only as a response to a stimulus. For example, they give a distinct alarm call for land and aerial predators, discriminating for the predator's size. These abilities help chickens navigate the dynamic network of social relationships they are involved with. They can recognize individuals internally and externally of their groups and recognize their own names.

Like many avian species, each individual hen shows a set of unique personality traits as documented by the people who spend a lot of time with them, such as on a small farm and in sanctuaries. Like humans, some chickens prefer solitude, and others enjoy company and are more fearless. They can be shy or bold and confident. It can also be differentiated for breeds as some will have a gentler temperament, and others, like Ancona, would be louder and flightier. In a flock, you can identify the bossy, sweet chick or the bright and thoughtful hen. For this, we can see chickens as complex individuals with multiple characteristics.

PIGS

Although it varies culturally, pigs are the second most consumed land animal globally. According to the Food and Agriculture of the United Nations Statistical Database, in 2020, there were 1,364,804,299 pigs slaughtered.

You might have a different emotional response to the previous sentence if I said there were a billion dogs slaughtered for chops and sausages each year. Elwood's Organic Dog Meat Farm is nailing it at showcasing this hypocrisy; check them out at https://www.elwooddogmeat.com/. There is no surprise that westerners are outraged by dog meat, yet at the same time, are very comfortable eating a rash of bacon daily. Both pigs and dogs are highly intelligent animals, while pigs sometimes can even exceed the dog's cognitive ability. Not appreciating this fact may be caused by moral dilemma and our personal preference to omit the information if it is calling for a change in our ingrained and comforting behaviour.

Domestic pigs show sophisticated social behaviour and naturally would live in groups of about eight individuals, benefiting from protection, nursing, and foraging activities. The Someone Project, which is a project sponsored by a sanctuary farm, published a research-based white paper, "Thinking Pigs: Cognition, Emotion, and Personality" [8]. The authors go in-depth about pig's memory and spatial learning, time perception, self-awareness, perspective taking, and more.

Research on pig intelligence also showed that they can have

long-term and preferential memory, prioritizing the site where more food was previously left. The sophisticated cognitive abilities are demonstrated by the presence of episodic memory, a phenomenon recently thought to be unique to humans. The pig can remember a specific event in their life for months or even years. They also can anticipate future events based on the past. As natural foragers, they also have an excellent spatial memory, able to remember where the food is located and its relative value, equivalently to the dog sniffing abilities.

When it comes to emotions, pigs not only are capable of feeling emotions, such as anxiety, fear, and joy but also exhibit emotional contagion, meaning they are capable of comprehending the emotion their mate is feeling. This is the basis for more complex emotions, such as empathy. Being highly vocal and social animals, their ability to comprehend the guests and verbal symbols should not be surprising.

I find it interesting that researchers have to prove that animals possess personalities and have different temperaments and unique behavioural traits. When you look at nature, you understand how diverse and unique it is, and each individual, plant, and insect have something of their own. This is incredibly easy to observe if you have a companion animal. My cat, for example, lets me know when he wants to play and will make a fuss if I am not paying attention. He is incredibly playful and extraverted as he loves to meet new people and would happily hop on their laps. Pigs similarly possess personality types such as agreeableness, extraversion, and openness. Being able to relate to pigs through a perception of who they are as an individual would help us as a society to stop their exploitation, forcing them to live in miserable conditions, denying them the chance to be themselves as the individuals they were meant to be.

The environment in an intensive farm, with inadequate space, odours (reek of animal waste), dust, and individual stalls, are detrimental to their being. The pigs will definitely not be able to live a happy life demonstrating full cognitive abilities while living in a metal crate, confined to lying and standing at most. This contributes to high-stress levels, aggression, and poor physical and psychological health.

CATTLE

According to the Food and Agriculture of the United Nations Statistical Database, in 2020, there 1,587,068,322 cattle were consumed. Cows, especially dairy cows, are often not given enough credit for their intelligence, mainly because of the reliance on the products such as dairy, beef, veal, leather, and labour for ploughing and pulling. We should not be surprised about the intelligence of cows as they are highly developed mammals with exceptional cognitive abilities and markedly different personalities rather than being a plodding herd, as often illustrated.

It is difficult to measure an animal's intelligence, and some of the species, such as cows, in comparison to dogs, get less attention from researchers simply by being regarded as a commodity. In fact, researchers' attention is usually aimed at making farming more efficient or practical for the human benefit. Nevertheless, through years of research, it was shown that cows display high levels of intelligence and emotional sensitivity. Even though most of the research that analyses cows' behaviour focuses on increasing or optimizing food production or other use as commodities, the neuroscientist Lori Marino and Kristin Allen have looked at and dispelled many of the myths associated with cows' behaviour [9].

From birth, calves undergo stressful and harmful conditions affecting their physical and mental well-being. For example, a common practice in the dairy industry is to separate calves from their mothers. The study has shown how this affects calves, who developed adverse cognitive reactions due to emotional stress, leading to a permanent change in the brain. In addition, their lives are miserable until death as they are transported to slaughter in overcrowded conditions with no water and starving.

It is a shame that, as a society, we let these animals suffer until their rather soon death. In fact, beef cattle are slaughtered in Europe at one or two years old. On the other hand, dairy cows are usually slaughtered when they have been entirely exhausted after consistent calving and lactation, which consequently is less profitable. This is generally after four lactations at five to six years in a well-managed farm. If not for the commercial farms, they would be able to live beyond twenty years [10].

Cows are very social animals and form lasting social bonds with their offspring and the herd members if permitted. They also have strong emotions, for example, cows can hold a grudge against each other. In addition, they can discriminate between individuals and differentiate between familiar versus unfamiliar individuals, which is the basis for social relationships. In the experiment, the authors used photographs of familiar and unfamiliar cows. The cows in the experiment could recognize familiar faces and use the previous social interactions as a base for the decision. Given the study was conducted with photographs, chemosensory mechanisms did not play a role in helping cows identify individuals [11]. Being social animals, they are competent in social learning by observing their peers and extracting behavioural patterns and consequences of specific actions.

Cows have a good memory and can learn and retain information about the complex maze for six weeks. They can also remember the association between objects such as a plastic food bucket and the food reward for up to a year. Although further research on cows' intelligence is necessary for us to fully understand and appreciate these animals in a similar context that other animals are understood, such as time perception.

SHEEP

According to the Food and Agriculture of the United Nations Statistical Database, in 2020, there were 1,435,589,687 sheep consumed. They were among the earliest animals domesticated for human use. The meat of the sheep is usually referred to as lamb, which is a sheep in their first year. Read a baby. If you were to see a picture of lambs, it would be those cute little ones frolicking in the fields during the springtime.

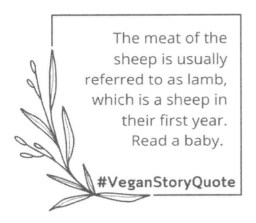

The meat of the sheep is usually referred to as lamb, which is a sheep in their first year. Read a baby.

#VeganStoryQuote

A common belief is that these animals are timid, unintelligent, and with no mind of their own. For this reason, they serve as linguistic metaphors for people who are viewed as blindly following *en masse*. Nevertheless, research reveals sheep possess individualistic traits, high cognition, and complex social behaviours, which is reviewed and neatly presented by Marino and Merskin [12].

Sheep are gentle and willing to be handled, which stereotypes them as simple-minded, unintelligent species. However, they possess some extraordinary skills. Being prey animals, they have an incredible vision and can see behind themselves without turning their heads. The smell and taste are also significantly developed, which helps them in mating and choosing preferable foraging areas.

Regarding social relationships, sheep can also identify the faces of different animals and have their preferences for familiar faces. Facial recognition is a complicated mental task, as we may know from Artificial Intelligence's efforts to replicate it. Sheep could remember and discriminate fifty faces, showing facial recognition and memory capabilities since this experiment was followed up for two years. Furthermore, sheep can also discriminate facial expressions representing emotions of fear, calm, and frustration. They experience and express complex emotions, including phenomena such as cognitive bias and the ability to demonstrate optimism and pessimism. One interesting experiment has shown that sheep can form an expectation [13]. This action required complex cognitive processing and the ability to extrapolate past events. Following the experiment where sheep were given a smaller reward than the expectation, thus not meeting them, the sheep responded emotionally as suggested by measuring the increased heart rate and movements.

Regarding personality, sheep's central dimension of character traits is shyness/boldness. The shy-bold dimension was determined by the studies aimed at demonstrating risk-taking, reactions to novelty, and levels of exploration. They also vary between individuals in their gregariousness, even though they are highly social animals as a group. Within such groups multifaceted and dynamic relationships can be found in a hierarchical order.

BEING HONEST WITH YOUR MORALS

There is no difficulty comprehending the difference between the carrot and the chicken. You would easily chop one taken straight from the farm but not the other. Likewise, the idea that non-human animals experience basic emotions (fear, anger, enjoyment, surprise, disgust, and sadness) is widely accepted. Needless to say, all these animals do not need to display any intelligence for us to justify our behaviour of breeding them into existence, exploiting them throughout their lives, and slaughtering them in a rather soon end.

Nevertheless, having a bit more understanding that animals feel complex emotions and are capable of sophisticated behaviour, it is only logical to follow through and understand that animals are just like us in many cases. They feel not only pain and suffering but are capable of loving, having fun, and feeling joy. They suffer separation anxiety and want to be cuddled and cared for. If you ever had a pet, you definitely can recognize it and most likely have powerful feelings for your companion animal. They come running to you when you return home and recognize your face. It doesn't have to be your dog or a cat, but this behaviour is also displayed in all other animals, including fish, chickens, geese, and horses. Unfortunately, for our personal convenience and comfortability, we have disconnected personalities and individualism from the farm animals, treating them no better than a piece of furniture. I must also add that it is not only about killing the animals, but the life experiences they go through due to outrageous practices disguised as animal welfare policies. Year after year, the incremental change of what we accept as standard has been shifting. For animal welfare, that means that practices unimaginable decades ago are currently a norm in many

It is time, to be honest with ourselves and our inner morals and see things for what they are.

#VeganStoryQuote

farms for efficiency and growing profits. One example is the farrowing crates, introduced in the 1960s for sows. They are cramped into these crates where no movement is possible just before giving birth. Imagine giving birth and then being confined to a tiny space with a perimeter the size of your body. In these crates, sows are unable to turn around and can barely stand, are not able to properly take care of their babies, and are forced to lie in their excrements.

It is time, to be honest with ourselves and our inner morals and see things for what they are. So here are some of the selected stories from people who truly love all animals beyond the socially acceptable cats and dogs.

🌿

After seeing a video on what happens to chicks, it pushed me to stop. We started eating most vegan meals for the first week, then I started disliking the taste of chicken thinking it tasted bloody, so the next week, we went full vegan. And it's been much easier than I thought. There are lots of really nice vegan substitutes to help you. We are now cooking more from scratch and eventually want to only have processed food once a week. I was surprised by how many things I liked.

🌿

I was part of an animal rights group in the 90s. I was vegetarian when I first joined, then I heard the new word vegan. I had not realized that dairy was as cruel as meat. So, I gave up dairy milk, then eggs cheese last. Being veggie made it easier as I was halfway there. I also changed my toothpaste, shampoo, and deodorant brands to vegan.

🌿

I am from a Japanese family with an overprotective mom - I saw sad stuff about animal testing on the Internet, so I boycotted stuff tested on animals and stopped eating meat at the age of 14. Crazy mother was so horrendous to me that I didn't let myself think about the whole animal agriculture until the age of 18. So when I saw a vegan's post about the egg industry - I wanted to go vegan, but she harassed me so bad I promised her I'd keep eating fish.

I couldn't deal with the guilt and sorrow for all the fish, so I went vegan after a few months. I studied until 10 PM at university every day with no food (university didn't have any vegan food), then cooked everything after everyone went to sleep so my mom wouldn't say nasty things to me. She eventually gave up and stopped being extremely vicious towards my veganism but always guilt-tripped me for "judging her" - when all I did was do the right thing for animals. I envy all the supportive family members some vegans have, but at the same time, I'm really happy for them because it really was hell.

I went vegan for animals almost three years ago after being vegetarian for about eight years. My only regret is I wish I'd done it sooner. But physically, I feel as fit as I did in my 30s and just turned 61.

I have been veggie most of my adult life and never knew about the dairy industry. I used to think that dairy cows had it easy. How wrong could I be?
I love the vegan life, and these days it's so much easier to choose plants over animals.

It's always been about the animals for me; I'm such a softie for them and believe we have a responsibility to take care of them. I just can't justify my five minutes of pleasure eating animal products to their lifetime of pain. I'll never go back.

I don't remember exactly how old I've been, but my first horrific encounter with animal cruelty was when I was riding home and saw a pig being slaughtered. I still remember there were three men, one of whom stabbed the poor animal. I didn't understand what happened, but the sounds shook me. It happened a second time when I was visiting my grandparent. This time I have remembered all the details and that horrific squealing.

The answers that my parents were trying to give were no longer enough. The explanation was that this is natural and normal and will provide for our family. I continued to ditch meat from my diet periodically, but growing up in a heavy carnivore family was difficult.

Nevertheless, those two stores haunted me and still haunt to this day. Eventually, I ditched all animal products and started a vegan lifestyle. I have watched several documentaries, too, and could no longer see myself any other way.

How to be vegan? First, connect with the animals and what they go through to end on our plates. Second, eat whole foods! Beans, greens, grains, lentils, fruits and vegetables, nuts, and seeds. UK shops have every meat and dairy substitute too!

I was vegetarian for five weeks and then went vegan. It is best to invest in some vegan cookbooks and make the usual meals, but veganising it.

I was veggie for a few years, and Vegan Sidekick comics called me out, so I went vegan.

Before going vegan, I had already been veggie for 20 years, so the first thing I did was a swap to plant milk. I preferred it in cereal, but I took coffee black for a few months. After that, I steered away from vegan cheese for a while, too, as it isn't (or wasn't) the same. However, vegan alternatives have significantly improved since I went vegan three and a half years ago.

Going vegan was pretty simple. Once I'd seen how we treat animals, there was no way I could justify continuing to support the animal agriculture industries. It's just so unnecessarily cruel, and besides, it's bad for your health and the environment too. So no going back for me. When you know you know.

I started by being a vegetarian. I was disgusted when I found out how long it takes to digest meat and for how long it sits in our digestive tract. A couple of years later, when I watched Earthlings and saw the reality of what is happening with farmed animals, I could not even look at milk, eggs, and other animal products. The talk by Gary Yourofsky confirmed that I made the right decision.

I changed because after seeing what animals have to suffer through, I couldn't keep helping it happen. Not to mention how much healthier it is and the environmental benefits. So don't worry about your family not becoming vegan with you; lead by example, and they'll likely follow!

I first went off eggs! Then I couldn't get the thought of people eating dogs out of my head. Whenever I had meat on my plate, I would push it to one side and think about dog meat. One day I was about to put a chicken in my oven, and I looked at my dog and thought, I'm a hypocrite. I went veggie. I then came across a video called Dairy is Scary, which just did it for me. I've been vegan for two years and honestly it's the best thing I've ever done.

✿

I was visiting Barcellona when I saw crabs with their price tags written on the shell. My partner remarked that it's as if prices were written on human heads. I'm not sure what happened, but I felt so sorry for those alive crabs. Since then, I didn't want any fish or meat. Thankfully where I live, there is plenty of choice for veggie and vegan foods available, so eating is easy both at home and out.

✿

I went from full meat lover to vegan on the 27th of December, 2018. I have been feeling guilty for years about eating poor animals; for some reason, that was my day. I have never looked back and never will. My heart, mind, body, and soul no longer carry the guilt of being responsible for the murder of animals.

✿

I'd been a vegetarian since 1973 when I was 16. I knew I didn't want to eat tortured, dead corpses anymore. I thought I was saving the planet by being vegetarian, but then a friend explained the cruelty surrounding dairy and egg industries, and at the age of 60, I went vegan overnight. That was 4 years ago. That was the best decision I've ever made.

✿

I cut out the dairy due to the horrific dairy industry before I cut out the meat.

✿

I saw an advert years ago for Beauty without Cruelty makeup - back when adverts that told the truth were allowed to be shown in the cinemas. The model's face disintegrated, just like the animal's, when testing products on them. So, I decided not in my name. I went home, opened my fridge, saw all the body pieces, and decided I couldn't be part of that anymore.

I initially became vegan because I no longer wanted to contribute to animal cruelty. However, addressing climate change and environmental concerns has become an even greater priority. I love the taste of meat and fish and miss it, but it's a minor inconvenience compared to the ethical benefits of a plant-based diet.

I was 100% influenced by the ideas of professor Gary L. Francione. He makes very logical and indisputable arguments.

Animal cruelty and contaminated food made me go vegan.

It was 1991, and I was 25. I'd been veggie since my teens, and my then boyfriend, now husband, adopted two kittens from a sanctuary where I later decided to volunteer.

A few other girls were vegan, and when I told them I was vegetarian, they said that's great, but what about the cruelty in the dairy industry? I hadn't really thought too much about it before. I'd always thought being veggie was enough. Mostly, I worried about alternatives (there weren't too many back then). Still, they introduced me to soya milk, limited other things such as veeze (a rubbery cheese substitute), carob chocolate, granose sausage mix, and dried soya grits, which you could make bolognese and shepherd's pie with. Soon after, the food range hit the market, which made life easier.

I went straight for it, and my other half followed a few years later. I've seen many changes and improvements over the past 30 years. I've never looked back or regretted it for a moment. Yes, I've missed certain foods, but it's a kinder and healthier way to live, so the benefits definitely outweigh the negatives.

My mum has been vegan for three years, and I've always tried her meals but kept saying, "I couldn't do it". Then I started feeling guilty every time I had meat, and then I randomly saw a PETA post with images from a slaughterhouse. So that day, I stopped eating meat. Then I still thought I couldn't give up cheese, but two months in, I decided I could, so I did. It's been six months, and I don't miss it a bit.

I have been inspired by the healthy, whole foods online store. However, I have delayed about a year since breastfeeding and didn't want to drastically change my diet. I later watched documentary videos such as Vegan, Hope, The Game Changers, etc. My last straw was one story about a pig who ripped their leg off while trying to escape death.

Gary Yourofsky's talk "Best Speech Ever" was what made me choose a vegan lifestyle.

I went vegan for every reason but mainly for the animals. I never look back, and it's so much easier than I expected it to be.

My health was declining, and I was feeling sorry for the animals. I have watched the Earthlings, Cowspiracy, and other documentaries. I then decided to completely remove all animal products from my life.

We went straight from heavy meat eaters to vegan on the 1st of May 2018. I bought the BOSH recipe book as we thought of giving it a go to see if it would help my partner's medical condition. We joined the vegan food Facebook group, read as much as possible, and asked for advice. We decided to try it for a day, just using the Bosh recipes, no pressure, and then see. We then did another day, and here we are - vegan for the animals because now we know what we never knew before! Still make all our favourite meals, too, just vegan... it's so easy once you get the hang of it.

One animal rights activist has advised watching the video of how animals are treated in the animal farming industry. Watch it without closing your eyes, living through all emotions, and without running away. You cannot ignore any of it after this experience.

4 VEGAN FOR HEALTH

Health is the soul that animates all the enjoyments of life, which fade and are tasteless without it.
Lucius Annaeus Seneca

We first must clarify that veganism is never about us or about our health. Veganism aims at minimising the suffering of the animals as much as it is practically possible. Nevertheless, there is a common belief that vegans eat healthy, such as salads, nuts, and fruits. But let me tell you, eating just salads will most likely deprive you not only of macronutrients such as protein but also calories, and you will feel anything but healthy. Incorporating a good source of protein such as lentils, tofu, and beans and packing the meals with seeds and nuts will make them more nutritious and wholesome. One of the experts in plant-based eating, Dr Michael Greger, has a dedicated website focusing on whole food plant-based (WHPB) nutrition, **www.NutritionFacts.org**, full of resources to help you choose the right balance and ingredients for your daily food intake.

When switching to veganism, be it for health reasons or otherwise, it is important to make it right and not just remove meat, eggs, and dairy from your ration without replacing necessary nutrients. In fact, this happens often, and we end up having disappointed "ex-vegans" who just didn't know any better. Thus, joining a vegan challenge or supportive groups on a social network, such as Vegan Food UK, reading information from a reliable source such as the one cited above will give you the necessary tools to keep healthy and immediately stop contributing to the atrocious industry of animal farming.

IS BEING VEGAN REALLY HEALTHY?

If we focus only on the food aspect of veganism, I would compare it to the question of whether having a gym membership makes you fit. It certainly does not! You've got to put in the work and hours in the gym first. Similarly, with veganism, you have to make the right choices if you wish for your vegan lifestyle to be compassionate for the animals and beneficial to your health.

If you have recently wandered to any supermarket, you have seen the plentiful vegan chocolate and ice cream options. Let's not forget all the accidentally vegan snacks, biscuits, and crisps. Various alternative meat products are also available, and the offer is constantly growing. It ranges from sausages to no-chicken Kiyvs. The cheese boards are also not to be forgotten. They can easily be part of your vegan diet with plentiful choice availability of various types, including some artisan cheese so that each food guru can satisfy their taste needs. To sauce it all up, there are vegan salad dressings and mayo with so many options for which you don't need to go to a specialized store as the known brands competing for your custom have it available in major supermarkets. Even egg mixes have been developed to make lush scrambled eggs. Anything you can think of, there is a vegan version of it. Yes, that means pizza, ice creams, and even fakon (bacon) rashes to complete the full-English breakfast to perfection. I guess this allows us to conclude that vegan food being healthy is far from the truth.

Nevertheless, removing all animal products from the diet could have an incredibly positive effect. Over half of vegans said they have improved digestion, sleep, and energy after switching to a vegan diet. Regarding overall health, 8.1 million people would not need to die prematurely if we switched to a vegan diet globally [14]. For the scale, to date (20/July/2022), the Worldometer (https://www.worldometers.info/coronavirus/) reports the number of deaths with COVID-19 pandemic is 6.4 million. That is a lot of human lives that can be saved in parallel with saving billions of animals only by switching to a more sustainable and compassionate way of living. If you ask me, it is a no-brainer to adopt a vegan lifestyle combined with whole food plant-based eating.

WHOLE FOOD PLANT-BASED DIET

Even though the shelves are filled with sugary, salty, and greasy vegan food options, the WFPB food could be superior and beneficial to your health, potentially adding many healthy years to your life. So, you can have the best of both worlds: doing no harm to the animals and taking the best care of your own body. At the end of the day, you only have been given one body to carry you till the end of your days, so it's better to look after it.

The BROAD study was a randomised controlled trial, meaning subjects were randomly selected into two groups. One was assigned a WHPB diet, and the other had no intervention (just a standard medical care) for three, six, and twelve months [15]. Researchers looked at the outcomes such as obesity, ischaemic heart disease, and diabetes. They reported a reduction in most risk factors, such as BMI and cholesterol. Interestingly, all were achieved without limiting the calorific content or mandating any exercise. It was done with only 65 subjects, however, a meta-analysis (a study of multiple smaller studies to show an overall effect of the specific intervention) with nine unique cohorts and a total of 698,707 participants studying the association between WHPB diet and a risk for cardiovascular disease was recently published [16]. Authors reported a lower risk for cardiovascular disease and coronary heart disease, but the confidence of the reduction of risk of stroke was not present.

The health topic at the forefront of the media in the past several years was COVID-19. So, what role does a plant-based diet play in protection against this disease? Studies reported that plant-based diets were associated with a lower risk of overall infection and moderate-to-severe COVID-19 and subsequent consequences [17], [18]. It was also shown to benefit in managing a long-covid, mainly due to the prolonged systemic inflammation seen in dairy and meat eaters [19]. For one thing, I am sure, is that if a plant-based diet was a pill, everyone would be lining up to get one!

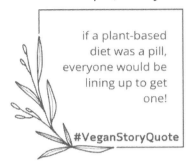

if a plant-based diet was a pill, everyone would be lining up to get one!

#VeganStoryQuote

Below you will read the stories from people who were choosing a vegan or a plant-based diet to primarily improve their health to discovering compassion for animals and the planet in their journey.

I was shocked by the documentaries What the Health and The Game Changers. That was the last straw for me. After that, I could no longer eat dairy and eggs as I was a vegetarian for four years. Later I became interested in climate change and our planet, and my veganism's purpose extended beyond my health.

I was vegetarian and had a suspected stroke at the age of 46. After lots of research, I cut out dairy too. The results were almost instant, and my health improved massively. I'm also a massive animal lover, so it made perfect sense to go vegan, and I wish I had done it years ago.
Bad cholesterol is only present in meat and dairy, so cutting that out is doing your health a huge benefit for starters, let alone the ethical reasons. I also did and recommend Challenge22; they're so supportive.

My daughter's health issues made us choose a vegan lifestyle. It has been 11 years, and I'm still joyful about it. Our life changed completely for the better.

I watched the video Forks over Knives on Netflix in January, which has changed my life. I never really liked veggies, but I have eaten mostly whole food plant-based (WFPB) since then. I don't call myself vegan.

Reading The China Study was enough for me to go vegan. I did it for health reasons.

What the Health documentary inspired me to go vegan.

I have been vegetarian for three years, almost vegan. Sadly, I am still learning things like wine has gelatin and how to read every label on food and ask restaurants questions about their ingredients. But it's been a wonderful transition. My fibromyalgia is almost nonexistent, I'm off all medication, lost weight, and my thought process is clearer.

I have a house full of carnivores, and I can honestly say it's very difficult. I feel they make fun of me and don't respect my beliefs. I am horrified at the meat/poultry/dairy industry and the abuse. My husband is in total denial and thinks it's instant and painless; it makes me feel so angry. But we will prevail one day, and all animals will live the lives they deserve.

I went vegan for health after watching The Game Changers. Then a few weeks in, I found out where my food came from and was horrified.

I have been a meat eater all my life until five months ago. I had my daughter two years ago, and every day since, I was sick whenever I ate or drank anything. Finally, my son (five years old) started to notice it and asked, "mummy do you need me to turn around so you can be sick". It broke my heart. From that day, I went vegan and haven't looked back. I don't miss meat or anything that isn't vegan; I wish I had done it sooner.

A worsened health made me think more about my diet. As a result, I became vegan the minute I finished watching the seminar by Gary Yourofsky. As a result, I now feel healthier than ever before.

I was a full-blown omnivore! Bacon sandwiches every day, meat with every meal. I was ignorant and taking the Mick out of vegans. I watched documentaries like the Game Changers, What the Health and Cowspiracy, and went plant-based. I watched Earthlings, Land of Hope and Glory, and Dominion and instantly went vegan.

I was vegetarian but wanted to be vegan. I was chatting to someone vegan in the US. I said I'd try it for a week because I wanted to eat better, and that was 9 and a half years ago!

My main reason for going vegan was health, specifically to help with eczema and fibroadenoma. Although my food journey was a rollercoaster, I found many rich tastes, clarity in the head, a mountain of energy, and a new way of life.

Three and a half years ago, I was working in London, where my breakfast each day consisted of milk and cookies, and lunch was five to six chicken legs with chips. Thanks to my father, I believed I must eat meat to be strong and healthy. I lived this lifestyle for four years until my health started crumbling, and the first thing to blame was the bad quality of meat I was consuming. Subsequently, I have started to eat less of it and included more vegetables.

After a YouTube video on spinach for health, I've found myself in a rabbit hole, researching veganism/raw veganism, scientific conferences, debates regarding human diseases, agriculture and earth resources, and animal rights.

I had no problem quitting meat and became vegan the next day. Firstly, it was for my health, but later I realized I would help myself and everyone else, giving me strength! I must say, my health really improved; I've retained my physical strength and increased my endurance.

I was trying to lose weight and read "Alan Carr's how to lose weight now". I did not expect it to be promoting plant-based eating at all. But I read it, and the way he puts it just makes sense. I started by cutting meat but not fish and some dairy. The cheese was the hardest, but I don't miss it now, and the thought of greasy pizza makes me sick! The transition became easier when I looked into how my food choices had affected animals - the documentary "Land of Hope and Glory" is a real eye-opener.

5 IT IS A WIN FOR ALL SITUATION

Our ability to reach unity in diversity will be the beauty and the test of our civilization.
Mahatma Gandhi

So far in this book, you have learned many different stories about why someone chooses to go vegan. You've read about vegans for health, although someone may insist, they are not vegans but just follow a whole food plant-based diet. You've read about vegans who choose it for the planet and ecology. But you've learned that eventually, people become vegan mainly for the animals. The eventuality of any reason behind the why is that animals and their excretions are not being consumed for food, entertainment, or clothing.

But let's agree on one thing, there isn't a better or worse vegan. If I had to choose between perfectionism and progress, I would vote for the latter anytime. As it was said many times, it is better to have millions of imperfect vegans than a handful of absolute idols. With our words and actions coming from empathy, we will achieve more, making a greater impact on the overall well-being of the animals. I applaud and congratulate each vegan who took this step regardless of the reason, as only by empowering and supporting each other will we make the world a better place for every kind. Regardless of your why vegans in any shape and form are actively not participating in the murder and exploitation of animals. That is the main goal, where everybody wins. Thus, no matter your vegan story, we are all united in making the planet earth a kinder and friendlier planet. Our ultimate goal, as vegans, is the same; first of all, we must be kind to ourselves and each other.

THE VEGAN WORLD

Let's paint the picture of what a vegan world would look like. I imagine it would bring peace to the earth. Peace of mind for the people who will be able to put their head on a pillow each night, knowing that their being alive did not cause suffering for others as practically as possible. It will bring peace to the animals going through unimaginable cruelty normalised over the history of industrial farming and beyond. Overall, compassion for all would increase, leading to a thriving planet. There would be more love, life, happiness, and joy. Being emphatic towards every kind would give more hope and exponentially increase joy in our lives.

Everyone, including young children, would be able to watch their nuggets or a burger made from start to finish without being traumatized due to the scenes of the slaughterhouse. Knowing that the food we eat or the shoes we wear are not part of the animal body with their own mind and life is the true peace that vegans strive for.

Besides anything else, I image a vegan community, the vegan world, as a healthier society that is more compassionate toward other beings and takes greater care of their health and well-being. I see a vegan world where eating a healthy plant-based meal is normalised and is a mainstream choice. It would also mean that we are not choosing to kill or abuse animals for their excretions or flesh, which eventually is making our own health poorer. Finally, I see a vegan world where the root causes of chronic illnesses and lifestyle diseases, such as type II diabetes or heart disease, are cured through appropriate food and lifestyle choices; rather than being stuck in a vicious cycle of causing harm to oneself, the planet, and the animals.

In a vegan world, we would seek solutions not based on greed and profits but rather sustainability, an increase in health and happiness. Being able to focus on what truly matters and strive to make the world better should be the primary cause, the profits and effectiveness of your system will eventually come as a side benefit. I promise, as witnessed in history, that if we want to find a viable solution, we can, and eventually, everybody will benefit. I am so thankful every day for all the inventions that have been made so far, making plant-based foods, textiles, and cruelty-free cosmetics accessible. I am grateful for the life we already have, and I believe the future is brighter and kinder. If you don't feel as optimistic, I recommend a book by Hans Rosling, a Swedish physician, academic, and public speaker, "Factfulness: Ten Reasons We're Wrong About The World – And Why Things Are Better Than You Think".

NO MISSING OUT

I truly love and enjoy being vegan. While writing this paragraph, I sit at a café, enjoying a wonderful oat latte and a scrumptious red velvet cake. Vegan, of course. Perhaps I am lucky to live in the part of the world where such things are easily accessible almost everywhere, but chances are that if you are reading this book, you have these options too. Being vegan does not mean missing out on family dinners or having lettuce when your friends enjoy a barbeque.

In the past three years since I became vegan, the offers have only been growing, and there is no sign that it will stop. Humanity is slowly coming to the sense that we do not need to breed a being into existence so that we can kill them while they have barely grown out of childhood. We can have all the taste and fun without the mad part of it. If you think otherwise, I'll just say, let's wait and see, but while we are waiting for the inevitable, why not be on the right side of history and "be the change you want to see in the world" – Mahatma Gandhi.

> Humanity is slowly coming to the sense that we do not need to breed a being into existence so that we can kill them while they have barely grown out of childhood.
> #VeganStoryQuote

In the second part of the book, through your stories, I will share the most common ways people become vegan, ranging from a natural transition from vegetarianism to going vegan overnight. Bear in mind that there is no right way, and each individual path depends on many circumstances, where one of the most important factors is how you learned about veganism.

PART II HOW

The problem in my life and other people's lives is not the absence of knowing what to do but the absence of doing it.
Peter Drucker

One could argue that how people become vegan is unimportant as long as they choose this path. Yet, understanding how someone did it makes it easier for others to know what to expect and provides valuable tips and tricks for making the best transition. It also enables animal rights activists to work in the right direction, focusing on specific guidance, activism, or tools that help people make this change smoothly.

As with all journeys, becoming vegan is the process and an emotional, informational rollercoaster. How you go through this journey makes a difference to your success in sticking with it, not feeling like an outsider, and most importantly, learning to eat sustainably, covering all nutritional requirements. The latter point needs addressing since vegans may get the bad rep from someone who tried "eating vegan for a week" and felt horribly merely due to lack of calories. The key here is that the switch is well-informed for long-term success. Many validated resources are available, including the fully balanced weekly meal plans. Those who fail to continue not eating animal products usually just remove the animal part from their diets without replacing it with appropriate caloric and macronutrient content, leaving a garnish on a plate. This undoubtedly will not keep you satiated and could lead to adverse effects.

Knowing how someone achieved the desired result does not automatically lead to success. Likewise, knowing the right thing to do does not always translate into taking the right action. We know all about the proper habits, yet seldom can we stick to them. We know that we must exercise, floss our teeth, and eat healthily, but only knowing doesn't make it any easier to have these habits ingrained in our daily routines. The information in itself isn't the power; it is the potential for the power, with a prerequisite to be acted upon it. Nevertheless, knowing how other people succeeded in transitioning to veganism not only provides practical information but also inspires and gives hope that you can do it too.

FOUR MAIN WAYS TO GO VEGAN

The key factor determining how you go vegan is how you found out about veganism in the first place. I mean, it is not a secret that some people choose not to consume animals in any way or form. Yet the rest of society is snoozing without realising how detrimental animal consumption is for the planet and personal health. Society fails to understand that farming is not about happy cows and smiley piglets but rather a real-life horror.

I have grouped the upcoming stories into the four chapters of the most common ways people go vegan. Of course, each story is unique, but those are the four general trends, so let's take a closer look at each.

A gradual transition is about taking it slowly, learning as you go along, and finding substitutes for favourite meals, snacks, and places to go out that at least have some good vegan options. It is sustainable as you can slowly replace items in your refrigerator and a snack drawer while not subjecting your body to a shock of an instant change.

Others jumpstart to veganism by already being vegetarian for years or even decades before the switch. This change is crucial as it marks the understanding of how dairy and egg industries are disguised as a cruel meat industry with added years of suffering and exploitation of the animals. If you currently are vegetarian for the animals, follow Chapter 7 closely.

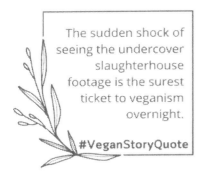

The sudden shock of seeing the undercover slaughterhouse footage is the surest ticket to veganism overnight.

#VeganStoryQuote

The sudden shock of seeing the undercover slaughterhouse footage is the surest ticket to veganism overnight. You cannot unsee the images; they may haunt you for years. Yet, meat-eating people often avoid these videos as deep down they know that facing reality may prompt them to make a change in their comfortable lives. So, if you haven't seen any, I challenge you to watch one documentary from Chapter 8, Vegan Overnight, about animal rights.

Finally, people go vegan simply through the influence or association with their family member or a good friend who wants to make a change but wishes to do it with someone they trust. Simply being with a friend who loves cooking and shares their tricks to making vegan banana bread will subconsciously lead you to mirror their actions. As the saying goes, show me your friends, and I will show you your future. Having the right influence in your life is one of the keys to sticking to good habits and leading a successful, fulfilling life, including becoming vegan.

6 GRADUAL TRANSITION

When we enter the spiritual realm, we are always focused on those big, life-altering miracles. Here is a truth that isn't sold to us. Change is a long, gradual process. Yes, you can make things happen immediately, but quite often, amazing things are happening that you can't see.
Ruben Papian

Becoming a vegan will always be a transition and a process. Some people need to take it slowly, making increment changes and adapting to their new lifestyle. It is absolutely fine and superior to jumping right in and then being unable to stay consistent.

STEADY AND CONSISTENT

Some people may choose to remove all animal products from their household immediately, be it donating the food to the family or even wasting it (which I think is not the best use of the resources already produced). Others would gradually eliminate one item after the other while consuming and sourcing a vegan alternative when required. With a latter approach, you have more time to accommodate your taste in the process and not shock the body with a sudden change. One of the great ways to make the transition seamless is by picking your favourite meal and learning how to make it all vegan. This way, you have a safe meal to return to when feeling discouraged.

There is one more advantage to choosing the incremental process. Your family and close friends can adapt to your new lifestyle, giving them time to learn about your new favourite treats or places to go out for a meal. It may seem trivial; however, it is vital to have people around you respect and understand your choices, and time enables the adjustment to be smoother. Perhaps you had a favourite cafe you used to go to with your family, and they, unfortunately, have no vegan options. This change will impact people around you, and hence to remove any resentment, allow some time to find a new ideal place you and your acquaintances could enjoy. The same applies to grocery shopping, especially if it is not you who does the shopping for the household. The incremental change will enable everyone to adapt better and support your evolution to veganism. Of course, there is an option to join you on the journey and together embark on the adventures in searching for a new family dinner recipe, vegan treats, and places to eat out.

Below are the stories of the people who took the slower, incremental approach in their journey to veganism.

The way I switched was by having a few vegan meals every week. Every payday, my partner and I would buy a couple of soya or almond milk, and after trying the Violife butter, we completely switched that.
Then in September, I became mostly vegan but only had fish occasionally. I then learned about fish farms and how bad they were, so I completely cut out fish to be a full vegan.
As a personal preference, I try not to have fake meats or high-fat or carby foods where possible and cook with as many fresh ingredients as possible.

I went veggie overnight when I was 14 years old. Since I have anaphylactic food allergies, the vegan transition was slower to ensure I could still eat a varied diet. I used up non-vegan foods in my cupboards and sourced vegan equivalents.

We gave up meat for lent, and my husband said we should exclude eggs too. Then we ate loads of cheese, which has never agreed with me. So, after a week, we decided to be vegan for the rest of lent, and we never looked back.

I thought about what I couldn't live without and spent time finding a substitute. For me, it was tea, and I needed to find suitable milk. I tried all the expensive ones, but cheap unsweetened soya won me over! And I also took the advice to give up on chocolate and cheese for a few months before trying vegan versions to help tastebuds adapt.

I transitioned to veganism slowly, over time. It took me about six months to make the complete switch, and that was six years ago with way less availability of vegan alternatives. One thing that helped me was that I was not looking for replacements, I was seeing if I could expect the new tastes, and now over time, I don't even remember what the other stuff tasted like. I turned vegetarian about 15 years ago, knowing my end goal was to turn vegan, and I needed to do it in a way that worked for me.

I had been vegetarian for several months and realised I didn't buy much dairy besides cheese and yoghurt. I had already switched to plant milk because I preferred it and only bought eggs for omelettes. I went on some retreats where the catering was vegan and realised that it wouldn't take much for me to substitute the remaining stuff and go vegan.

I decided to eat vegan once a week and then attended a vegan workshop. Occasionally I gave in to cheese cravings, but then I watched some heartbreaking documentaries about the dairy industry, and then it was easy to give it all up.

I had a charming vegan colleague when working in Germany one summertime. At that time, I'd been vegetarian for about a year. I was interrogating her about why she chose this lifestyle that looked so exotic and incomprehensible to me then. I thought being vegan was very difficult and required many resources.

She mentioned the horrible dairy industry practices and animal products influence our health. However, we had no chance to dwell deeper into this topic. Nevertheless, the seed was sown, and I started researching veganism a bit more until I realised I had removed all the animal products from my life.

I had been veggie for about ten years, and for health reasons, I started eating fish again, then meat. I ate like that for years but couldn't shake the feeling of guilt for the animals and the environment. Finally, I realised the "health reasons" I cited weren't so much to do with the fact that I wasn't eating animals but that my diet was terrible whether I was following a vegetarian or carnivorous diet.
I, therefore, transitioned to vegetarianism again by cutting out meat, fish, dairy, and eggs to follow a vegan diet, this time eating better. The final step was to look beyond my diet and choices about other products such as clothing, cosmetics, etc.

I was vegetarian for five weeks and then went vegan. It is

best to invest in some vegan cookbooks and make the usual meals, but veganising it.

It was a lockdown due to the COVID-19 pandemic, and we were tight on money because of double furlough and then double job loss. So, we stopped buying meat because it was too expensive. We then realised everything we made was accidentally vegan, so we just carried on.

I was veggie for a few years, and Vegan Sidekick comics called me out, so I went vegan.

Before going vegan, I had already been veggie for 20 years, so the first thing I did was a swap to plant milk. I preferred it in cereal, but I took coffee black for a few months. After that, I steered away from vegan cheese for a while, too, as it isn't (or wasn't) the same. However, vegan alternatives have significantly improved since I went vegan three and a half years ago.

I accidentally watched "Peaceable Kingdom" as the cover looked like it would be a beautiful movie. It still was nice, but it also made me think. I cried. Something happened inside of me that after that movie, I knew I was no longer going to eat any animal. With further information and being part of the vegetarian community, I slowly and naturally transitioned to veganism.

I have always preferred flora to butter and don't like eggs or any dairy aside from cheese, so I stopped buying cheese for a while before starting on vegan cheese. I looked at any label of things I got before I bought them and just found it so ridiculous that eggs and milk were put in products that seemed so unnecessary. It's a learning curve. I found recipes purely just made with veg and love cooking and experimenting. The more I look into how wrong meat and dairy are for the animals, us, and the planet, being vegan just makes more and more sense.

I started by being a vegetarian. I came across an animal rights website and became part of their online community, which subsequentially influenced my behaviour. I felt that I wasn't consistent in my action and thus slowly transitioned to being fully vegan.

I started thinking about what I was eating, and it got to the stage where I just felt sick, so I stopped eating animal products. I found it easy too. I'm a little over two years vegan now from a full omnivore.

I transitioned to veganism after watching The Game Changers and PETA's secretly filmed videos from slaughterhouses. It affected me psychologically, and it's been a year since I stopped eating meat. It smelled of corpses; I couldn't even look at it. So now I'm removing dairy from my diet too.

I watched a documentary, Forks over Knives, which brought up many questions, such as why do I eat meat if it is not necessary for me? It led to further research and understanding that I no longer want to participate in animal cruelty, destruction of Earth, etc. I have become more conscious.

Remembering myself, I was always an animal lover, loved watching National Geography, and veganism was just a question of time. Well, better later than never.

I went veggie at around 12 years old when I fully realised what I was eating. I met my partner, and he was a big animal eater until one day, he realised he didn't want to eat meat. We then transitioned really slowly to veganism after looking into it and watching documentaries etc. It started about three years ago by cutting out cows' milk and then cutting out cheese, and the hardest for us was cakes and chocolate. I would never look back now, though, and don't miss anything at all.

In my childhood, I had some vegetarian friends, but I used to bully them as I couldn't understand how one could live without Lithuanian "cepelinai", BBQ, hamburgers, and other meaty foods. All my family ate was dairy and meat; thus, I grew up with this same mentality and habits.

Around the age of 16 to 17, I have come across a video of animal cruelty in the farming industry. I didn't even watch it; the title was enough. I've shared it with my friend, who stopped eating meat from that day. However, I kept eating all the meaty pizzas and sausages.

Time passed, and I became more conscious about my health and eating habits. I've started volunteering and helping animals and also watched Gary Yourofsky's video about veganism. It wobbled my head, and I stopped eating meat the same day. Slowly I've removed eggs and dairy too. Now I live a very happy life!

First, I started reducing processed meat products, then started following some animal rights organisations on social media. Finally, I have experimented with my cooking, trying to make dishes, first meatless and then without other animal products.

The most inspiring was a video by Gary Yourofsky, followed by the book How Not to Die by Dr Greger.

I did it gradually, so I wasn't too hard on myself. I wasn't a vegetarian before, so it was a giant leap. I just instantly cut meat out, but I was more relaxed with dairy. It needs to be a transition; it doesn't matter if you have a brew with milk in it if that's the only thing available. It takes time, sometimes a year, to find your way.

Once I've eaten some amazing veggie food and realized I did not need to eat carcasses. So, after a reasonably short time, I planned ahead, went to the supermarket, and became vegan.

7 VEGGIE TO VEGAN

Our task must be to free ourselves… by widening our circle of compassion to embrace all living creatures and the whole of nature and its beauty.
Albert Einstein

Why this chapter, you ask? Isn't vegans and vegetarians the same? Well, in one word: no. Have you ever come across the terms vegan and vegetarian used as synonyms? Although it may seem obvious, it is not always easy to distinguish between veganism and vegetarianism for people outside the veganism bubble. For simplicity, I will only focus on food and leave the rest of the veganism aspects on the side for now. The terms are often used interchangeably by our close circle and mislabeled in catering establishments. I have once been served a clearly labelled vegan full English breakfast only to see that there were real chicken eggs on my plate upon its arrival. It only shows that it is necessary to educate society on what veganism is and what exactly vegans eat, and how that differs from vegetarians or even pescatarians. A simple example: I am in the process of planning a wedding, and the venue has both vegan and vegetarian options, but if you look at the vegetarian meals, they have shrimps and sea bass. The last time I checked, those were animals! Don't be surprised if you are a vegetarian and get served seafood in different parts of the world.

WHAT EXACTLY IS THE DISTINCTION?

Vegetarians simply omit animal flesh from their diets; this will always include meat and fish. Others will also choose to exclude dairy or eggs. Veganism, on the other hand, is a much deeper approach to excluding animals for the human benefit (or detriment as we know it now). Vegans refuse to use animal products in other ways, such as for entertainment, zoos, clothing, and other industries. I must emphasise that the above does not apply if no other option is possible, such as getting the required/life-saving medicine even though they contain gelatin, for example. Nevertheless, it doesn't stop us from advocating for researchers to find more sustainable alternatives to be used in medicine, reconsider laboratory animal testing, and such.

So next time someone says they are vegan, don't be quick to offer them milk chocolate or eggs benedict for brunch; however, nowadays, the choice of animal-free options is plentiful to find.

NATURAL TRANSITION

Many vegetarians refuse to eat animal flesh for ethical reasons. The marketing of happy cows and joyful chickens in the egg industry makes it easy to believe that dairy cows, and egg-laying hens, particularly male chicks, have a wonderful life surrounded by green fields and sunshine. That picture could not be further from the truth! From an animal point of view, both dairy and egg industries are disguised meat industries where animals are subject to many more years of cruel life and exploitation. Babies, especially males, are often killed as deemed unprofitable to keep them, and females are redirected to the misery of egg or dairy production.

It is only logical for vegetarians who choose this lifestyle out of love for animals and their well-being to go vegan as soon as they know the truth behind dairy and eggs. Some vegetarians are learning this information and getting

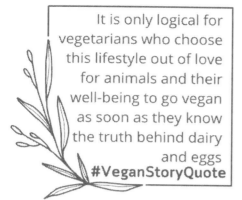

It is only logical for vegetarians who choose this lifestyle out of love for animals and their well-being to go vegan as soon as they know the truth behind dairy and eggs
#VeganStoryQuote

educated about the horrors in the egg and dairy industries, thanks to the documentary makers and animal rights activists. Becoming vegan for ethical reasons is the next most logical and practical step. Unfortunately, it may take many decades or just a couple of months after figuring out how easy it could be to replace all non-vegan products in your household.

In the stories below, people share what it took them to realise the difference between vegetarianism and veganism, how long it took, and if it was any more different from being vegetarian.

Going vegan was a natural transition from being vegetarian. Milk went first, eggs last. I never looked back; it was the best decision I ever made.

Been vegetarian on and off for some years and then decided to go back to vegetarianism four and a half months ago. I have then watched something that made me decide to become vegan overnight. So I've now been vegan for three months and 25 days!
My partner, who was always a meat lover and had always said he wouldn't go vegetarian, has also been vegan for three months and 25 days.

I came upon an animal rights stall and saw the horrors of

meat sourcing. I went veggie overnight. That was 20 years ago. A couple of years ago, I ditched animal by-products and dairy.

❧

I have been veggie for over two decades and had never heard of a chick macerator. As soon as I did, I went vegan instantly.

❧

I was a vegetarian for 13 years from the age of eleven. Then, in 2016 I found out more about the dairy industry, and from then on, I have decided to go vegan, cutting out the cruel toxic products. I'll never look back.

❧

I was veggie for over 25 years, not realising the horror of dairy and the egg industries. When I finally woke up to the atrocities, I completely stopped and just cut it all out. With so many vegan options, it was easy, and plant-based milk tastes much better than tittie milk!

❧

I went vegan since the two weeks juice cleansing program seven years ago. It cleared up eczema I had had all my life. I have been a vegetarian since 1985.

❧

I wanted to increase my physical vibrations before one powerful spiritual practice, and thus I've practised veganism for two months. I absolutely loved it; I felt as if I had more energy, my skin got more beautiful, the sweat got odourless, and my body produced less mucous. Well, in short, I liked it all and never got back to dairy products. Before that, I have been vegetarian for 20 years.

Having looked into why vegan instead of just veggie, I did not put another mouthful of non-vegan food into my body — the End.

I was a vegetarian for over thirty years; I drank soya but still ate eggs, cheese, butter, etc. Then I joined a local Facebook group where most members were vegan, discovered the horrors of the dairy and egg industry, and then gave up honey. I've been vegan for eight years and wish I'd done it so much sooner.

I was a vegetarian for 36 years, so someway there. To make the switch to veganism easier, I joined many groups and hung out with established vegans, looked in their cupboards, went to a couple of Pot Lucks, and watched a lot of YouTube!

I was veggie for about 35 years with periods of no dairy or eggs anyway. So the last to go was eggs; even though I hated the taste, I thought I needed them nutritionally. Without fully knowing what I was doing, I got very sick the first time I did vegan, but then I eventually trained as a vegan educator, so I learned everything and started to love cooking!

I decided 13 years ago to go vegan, but it would be much easier today. I switched to vegetarian initially back in 1995. My wake-up call was after seeing a film called "Animals Film", which was solely about animal cruelty. Health was never a consideration and still isn't. The environment is also a consideration. There are so many food options today, and it's easier than ever.

I had been vegetarian for 40 years but wanted to go full vegan because the milk industry slaughtered male calves so that we could use milk. The ideology was there.

My first issue was the proteins until I realised that getting protein wasn't an issue. Then, a friend recommended the book "Proteinaholic" By Garth Davis, MD. He writes about the myths of protein and how as a society, we over-consume protein.
The second strand was a friend who cooked vegan at home but ate vegetarian when eating out. I felt "I can do that", which was a good bridge point for me. However, as I got more into it, I decided that I wanted to be 100% vegan, even in restaurants, despite the inconvenience at the time.

The third strand, I have been a type 2 diabetic since 2010. A friend recommended "Reverse Diabetes Diet" by Dr Neal Barnard. It's a vegan diet that is low in fat but places no restrictions on carbohydrates.
Within three months, my diabetes medication was cut by half, and another three months later, I completely controlled diabetes by diet alone.

My sister sent me a video. I didn't watch, all it took was to hear a pig screaming for one second. I've owned a slaughterhouse, and I've seen and heard animals being slaughtered many times, but it has never affected me as much as that video did.

Nevertheless, I have been trying to go veggie on many occasions, yet never successfully. However, that video suddenly opened my eyes. I have instantly become a vegetarian and must admit a fierce one. I was advocating for everybody to quit eating meat, and I fought for animal rights, continuing for four and a half years.

I then came across the pagan religion and found a new love for life and the world. It made me realise humanity's purpose here on Earth and start accomplishing it. However, enormous sadness took hold of me one day, thinking I was only a tiny parasite on this Earth, using the resources without returning anything. I then realised that I could be the change, and while on this Earth, I must not destroy her, being a conscious consumer, not living at anyone else's cost.

Around six years ago, my acquaintance shared the "Farm to Fridge" documentary, and my reaction to that was, why would they use animals as if they are objects? Why do they keep them in such cramped cages?

It made me think about whether it is possible to live without eating meat. Of course, a quick google search revealed that it is perfectly possible. I then started to practice pescetarianism, now fully understanding that it was a bit speciaistic of me. I've watched Gary Yourofsky's seminar on YouTube in five years, thus entirely removing dairy from my menu.

After 15 years of vegetarianism, one hour of Gary Yourofsky's talk changed my life. I would never go back again; it's been over five years now that I am vegan.

We were veggie for decades but lying to ourselves about eggs and dairy, saying and believing it didn't really harm the animals. I feel pretty stupid; really, vegetarianism is pretty pointless when I look back.

Like many, I have also started my journey from being a vegetarian, which lasted for four years. It took me further research into the industry to find out how animals are exploited, to go vegan. After that, the use of animal products became unreasonable.

I have been a vegetarian for ten years without overthinking about it. It is because I never really liked eggs, and dairy was getting a bad reputation regarding health, and I slowly shifted away from dairy products.

I have joined several vegan groups on social media, mainly for recipes, and watched a few documentaries, after which there were no doubts that I would like to lead a vegan lifestyle. My only regret is that I didn't realise it sooner.

My veganism journey started with me being a vegetarian for 14 years. It was quite easy to become vegan with all the abundant alternatives available at the stores. After my son's birth, I went vegan without much thought; it happened naturally.

I have been a vegetarian for 22 years as I was raised this way. I think it is easy to switch to veganism when researching comfort meals.

I started cutting down on dairy (after being vegetarian for 20 years) last autumn and went strictly plant-based at the new year - after a Christmas gorge on chocolate and mince pies.

I was vegetarian for five weeks and then went vegan. It is best to invest in some vegan cookbooks and make the usual meals, but veganising it.

I was veggie for a few years, and Vegan Sidekick comics called me out, so I went vegan.

Before going vegan, I had already been veggie for 20 years, so the first thing I did was a swap to plant milk. I preferred it in cereal, but I took coffee black for a few months. After that, I steered away from vegan cheese for a while, too, as it isn't (or wasn't) the same. However, vegan alternatives have significantly improved since I went vegan three and a half years ago.

8 VEGAN OVERNIGHT

Sometimes it takes years for a person to become an overnight success.
Prince

Most people who cut out all animal products immediately have seen a documentary on animal farming or a video clip from a slaughterhouse that has affected them so deeply that they could no longer get back to consuming the meat. In fact, "if slaughterhouses had glass walls, everyone would be vegetarian", said Sir Paul McCartney. Although, the walls are not see-through, and we as a consumer society choose to turn a blind eye to the horrors that happen inside the slaughterhouses. Willful blindness is the biggest enemy of those baby animals brought to this world to live in horror and die too early.

Thankfully, the information on animal agriculture, plant-based meals, speciesism, and many other topics associated with veganism is plentiful and can be easily accessible. In addition, the selection of available documentaries is extensive and constantly growing. Here is a carefully sourced list of the most impactful ones, separated into animal rights, health, and environment categories. It is not strict grouping, and some documentaries touch on several different topics.

DOCUMENTARIES: ANIMAL RIGHTS

- 73 Cows. The story of the first farmer in the UK to trade beef farming for sustainable organic vegan farming, giving up his entire herd of cattle in the process.

- Akashinga: The Brave Ones. The all-female anti-poaching unit in Zimbabwe is revolutionising how many of Africa's key species that are near extension are protected.
- Blackfish. The documentary explores the controversy of the captive orcas.
- Dairy is Scary. It is a short, five-minute video into why the dairy industry is inherently cruel.
- Dominion. It contains a hidden camera and aerial footage of the animal agriculture practices, focusing on farmed animals, wild animals, companion animals, entertainment animals, fur animals, and animal experimentation.
- Earthlings. Hidden cameras are employed to explore the practices of the industries that depend on animal exploitation, including entertainment, food, and clothing.
- Eating Animals. Examines the food we put in our bodies and how it changed from the traditional farming communities to massive industrial farming complexes.
- Food, Inc. The documentary paints the picture of America's controlled food industry, usually at the price of health and safety (of the food itself, of the animals produced, of the workers on the assembly lines, and the consumers eating the food) seeking to increase profits, producing the cheap food.
- Gunda. The film follows the daily life of a sow and her piglets, two cows, and a one-legged chicken, questioning our relationship with food.
- Land of Hope and Glory. It exposes the hidden truth behind animal farming in the UK.
- Live and Let Live. The feature documentary examines our relationship with animals, the history of veganism, and the ethical, environmental, and health reasons that move people to go vegan.
- Okja. This action-adventure film features a girl on an adventure to rescue her genetically modified pig,

whose fate is in the meat industry.
- Peaceable Kingdom. This documentary is about several farmers who refuse to kill animals and how they convert to veganism as a way of life, creating an animal sanctuary.
- The Cove. Undercover animal rights activists expose the cruel acts against wild dolphins.
- The End of Meat. The film envisions a future where meat consumption belongs to the past. It reveals the hidden impact of meat consumption, explores the opportunities and benefits of a shift to a more compassionate diet, and raises critical questions about the future role of animals in our society.
- The Milk System. A critical look at the milk system, questioning its assumed health benefits. The documentary features farmers, dairy owners, politicians, lobbyists, NGOs, and scientists.

DOCUMENTARIES: HEALTH

- Fat, Sick, Nearly Dead. The 60-day journey of an overweight man suffering from autoimmune disease towards better health taking advantage of fruit and vegetable juices.
- Forks Over Knives. Researchers explore the possibility that people changing their diets from animal-based to plant-based can help eliminate or control diseases like cancer and diabetes.
- Hungry for Change. The documentary exposes the secrets of the food, diet, and weight-loss industries and how people are deceived through aggressive marketing strategies.
- In Defense of Food. Documentary answering the questions of how the modern diet has been making us sick and what we can do to change it.
- Meat me Halfway. This film explores the practical,

reductarian path to going plant-based.
- The Game Changers. Explores the benefits of plant-based eating, focusing on endurance, strength, and protein.
- VEGAN 2020 – The Film. It covers the ever-growing vegan movement and how it's best for the animals, human health, and the planet. Fun fact; as a scientist working on COVID-19 research, I was featured in this documentary for almost two seconds, pipetting at the University of Cambridge.
- Vegucated. It is a guerrilla-style documentary that follows three meat- and cheese-loving New Yorkers who agree to adopt a vegan diet for six weeks and learn what it's all about.
- What the Health. The documentary explores the link between our diet and diseases.

DOCUMENTARIES: ENVIRONMENT

- An Inconvenient Truth. The documentary seeks to raise public awareness about the climate change threat to the Earth.
- Before the Flood. Dangers of climate change and the possible solutions are investigated, featuring Leonardo DiCaprio, who is meeting experts in the field.
- COWSPIRACY: The Sustainability Secret. This is an environmental documentary investigating the most destructive industry when it comes to our planet.
- David Attenborough: A Life on Our Planet. A powerful documentary, a scientist's testimony on the dramatic changes over a lifetime created by the accumulating damage to our planet over two centuries of intensified extraction and consumption of natural resources.
- Eating Our Way to Extinction. The journey around the world, documenting the ecological collapse through

testimonials, accounts, and renowned experts in the field.

- Honeyland. The documentary of a loner beekeeper of wild bees. Some topics explored are climate change, biodiversity loss, and exploitation of natural resources.
- I am Greta. Journey alongside the climate change activist who is trying to get people to listen to the scientists about the world's environmental problems.
- Inhabitants. It is a feature documentary that follows five Native American Tribes across deserts, coastlines, forests, and prairies as they restore their traditional land management practices.
- Kiss the Ground. The documentary focuses on animal extinction, water supply, and climate change and how replenishing the soil helps solve the above issues.
- Our Plant. Series that will take you to experience the planet's natural beauty through an examination of how climate change impacts all living creatures in this ambitious documentary of a spectacular scope.
- Rotten. This docuseries travels deep into the heart of the food supply chain to reveal unsavoury truths and expose hidden forces that shape what we eat, exposing the corruption, waste, and real dangers behind your everyday eating habits.
- SEASPIRACY. The impact of the fishing industry on the world's oceans.

These documentaries are a good source of information, covering the broad aspect of veganism, from our health to the impact of animal farming on climate change. However, some are extremely disturbing and are hard to watch. You could easily choose not to watch The Dominion; however, animals do not have that luxury of choice and live through hell as you peacefully read this sentence. Our brain will try to block this information as it is not what we want to see and remain in blissful ignorance. Nevertheless, I hope you give at least some of these documentaries a chance if you haven't already and fill yourself with not only the information but also passion and hope for a better future.

MAKING THE COMMITMENT

It's important to understand that while an hour of a documentary may give you some motivation, it could be short-lived, and the excitement will be put on the back shelf. It is, therefore, important to become part of the bigger community and join a vegan challenge (more on this later on) where you may get counselling, support, and, most importantly, a sense of belonging. Besides, most of these campaigns will offer an excellent resource for vegan meal ideas and other tips on making small changes in everyday life to remove animal products and consequently be part of the movement reducing animal exploitation.

It is common to go vegan cold turkey after watching or even hearing the above documentaries, particularly concerning animal rights. In fact, a few minutes of the footage of how some animals are handled behind the doors of a slaughterhouse have sufficed for many current vegans.

Any vegan will tell you that becoming one is more straightforward than they once thought.

#VeganStoryQuote

It may seem more challenging to make a change in the beginning than it actually is. Any vegan will tell you that becoming one is more straightforward than they once thought. Once you commit to yourself and don't look back, your brain helps you look for and find the solutions you never thought about. Find out from vegans themselves how they went vegan cold turkey and never looked back.

I went vegan 'cold turkey' just eight weeks ago from literally meat eating, alcohol, and caffeine to now - vegan, fasting one day every week, no caffeine or alcohol. It was for many reasons, including spiritual ones, to get clarity and be the light following the 'Essenes' way of living and being.

For me, ethical reasons were the most influential to becoming vegan. Mostly the documentary "Earthlings". I went from being an omnivore to vegan overnight, and so did my family. It was neither hard nor feeling weak, and any sighting of animal products makes us cringe, as we know how they were "made".

Veganism turned my world upside down, made us open our eyes, and removed the pink shades, pushing me further to appreciate many things. My goals and mindset also changed. Becoming vegan was my life's best decision, and I regret not making it sooner.

I became vegan overnight after watching a video "If slaughterhouses had glass walls" by Paul McCartney. Before that, I was a complete omnivore for 50 years and 11 months. So, if you ever find yourself faltering, think of the animals. You'll never regret going vegan.

I've become vegan after accidentally watching the documentary "Peaceable Kingdom: The Journey Home". I thought it was about humans and their animals' love, and it turned out to be very cruel, touching me deeply. It was a story about farm animals and their individual life experiences. At that point, I understood that I am the one who contributes to the hell animals go through only because of the lack of understanding. I howled my eyes and knew I would never eat meat again. That same day, my husband joined me in this new idea.

I subsequently did thorough research and learned more

about animal rights, their problems, and the impact of animal farming on our health, planet, and ecology.

I became vegan quite simply overnight, 16 years ago. I just stopped eating meat and dairy. Soya milk was something I had to get used to, but it's fine after a few weeks.

Today, everything is so easy. There are so many vegan products out there. The cheese wasn't good back then, and the mock meat wasn't that great. Today, it's come on so much.

I became vegan overnight after watching Dairy is Scary on YouTube. I had no idea of the cruelty in the dairy industry. I thought I was doing well not eating meat. I did eat fish, though, so I gave that up too.

I found to stop consuming milk and cheese the hardest, which is pretty much the same for everyone. But your tastebuds adapt in 21 days, according to Challenge 22.

I was vegetarian from 12, unfortunately, for only six weeks. I watched Cowspiracy when I was 15. It made me immediately research further, and I went out and did a vegan shop. I haven't looked back since.

I went vegan overnight in an attempt to improve my health - which worked instantly. Then I further educated myself about the other benefits for animals, the planet, and our health.

I had no idea what vegan was some 15 years ago. I thought

it was a planet. I just watched the documentary "Earthlings" and knew I could never support the exploitations I just witnessed.

I just thought about the cruelty inflicted on animals in animal agriculture and went vegan.

I became vegan overnight from watching a documentary. My husband has been vegan for over ten years. It's easy if you commit. Now that we are expecting, our babies will also be vegan.

We went vegan all in after watching the documentary Forks over Knives —17 months in and loving it.

I went vegan overnight. I gave away foods I would no longer eat and re-did my shopping. I have never looked back.

I went vegan overnight! I set a date (the day after my birthday meal so I could still have a birthday cake) and planned a week's worth of meals.

I went vegan overnight and never had a problem!! Before that, my diet was heavy in meat and dairy! Best thing I ever did, and I wish I had done it sooner!

I watched Vegucated on Netflix. Lightbulb moment, straight

from carnist to vegan. That was six and a half years ago.

I committed to eating plant-based on one day a week. But, after my first day, I just never went back.

For me, there's a point at which you say "no more". Then it doesn't matter whether you've changed a day, a week, a month, or a minute ago. You don't go back.

I just woke up one day after considering becoming vegan for years, took myself into the shop, and looked for vegan options for all the alternative products that I thought I would miss as a vegan. I came home and told my partner that this is the day I don't feel forced to start it but want to begin to eat as a vegan. He said Okey and has made me the most wonderful vegan food ever since.

I've got a cat, and he saved my life. I knew there was a disconnect between loving him and loving animals in general while still eating them. I went from eating meat to becoming vegan overnight. I'm now more mindful of the products I wear/ use too and opting for more vegan-friendly ones.

I went vegan overnight 30 years ago. I have been a vegetarian since the age of 11. Again, an overnight decision to give up all meat and fish. For me, it was always for the animals. I wish I'd gone vegan from childhood.

I became vegan overnight from watching a documentary. My husband has been vegan for over ten years. It's easy if you commit. Now that we are expecting, our babies will also be vegan.

STEREOTYPICAL VEGAN

We, humans, tend to reject anything that is not like ours or not familiar. Vegans are still a tiny proportion of the population. Most people reject it without opening their minds to abolish the preconceived ideas of what it takes to be a vegan. Rejecting veganism often comes from the fear of being an outsider and has nothing to do with the true feelings stemming from our inherently compassionate hearts.

It is common to think that a vegan diet is bland and restrictive. Still, there are too many stories to ignore that becoming vegan, people opened their eyes to more tastes of the world, found unique, unexplored cuisines, and even discovered foods they never knew existed. A great example of this would be the nooch, a.k.a nutritional yeast, tempeh, and the deliciously creamy oat milk in a coffee. In addition, many discovered their culinary skills by simply being willing to try and replicate some of the favourite dishes they used to have. Not to mention that all the spices are inherently plant-based, so to think that vegan food is bland is the highest form of ignorance.

to think that vegan food is bland is the highest form of ignorance.

#VeganStoryQuote

Another sad stereotype is that vegans are militant, extreme, overly passionate, and self-righteous, stuffing their agenda down everyone's throat. Yes, we get a bad reputation, but the truth is that far more, and I mean the vast majority are kind people, ready to bake you the most delicious vegan brownie for inspiration. It is also true that many people don't even know any single vegan from their bubbles and thus could only make a connection with the ones that are loudest or painted by the mainstream media as extremists for more clicks and likes. From a curious omnivore's perspective, it could be daunting to be trying your best and willing to make a change to be suddenly policed by the perfect vegans. Still, I vote for progress over perfectionism every time as it will bring more benefit in the long run. It's important to feel within yourself that what you do is the best you can and keep it true to yourself, aligning what is in your heart and what is on your plate. Yet many current vegans are thankful that someone brave has made them aware of the reality.

On the other hand, people think of vegans as tree-hugging, meditating, spiritual humans. And while it is incredible, not every vegan meditates in the morning, fermenting their kombucha or growing a community herb garden.

Whatever the stereotypes you may hold, the best place to start breaking them would be to meet real people and listen and hear their stories. Vegans come in all shapes and forms, all ages and walks of life from across the globe living in different cultures.

NOTHING HAPPENS OVERNIGHT

Although this chapter is named vegan overnight, it is more likely than not that anyone who had become vegan overnight had the seeds of veganism growing inside of them for way longer. Perhaps the seed of compassion was planted in childhood when watching your uncle kill the chickens by snapping their necks or the short video from an inside animal farm you've accidentally seen.

A profound love for animals is ingrained in us. It is a moral choice best aligned with our inner values. With some deviations, no one wants animal suffering and would smile seeing a chick pecking on some grains or a grazing sheep in a field. The fact that we inherently love animals but at the same time do not connect what is on our plate means that somewhere along our lives, we will stumble across little pieces of the puzzle connecting to our true values. It will help us fully realise that we have immense power with each meal we have. This moment is when a person becomes a vegan overnight.

If you have made the connections between the meal you have and the animal you love, perhaps while eating a steak and petting your dog and looking at their affectionate eyes or visiting a sanctuary farm, the best step is to take part in the vegan challenge. Although it is not strictly an overnight adventure, joining a challenge is a great way to transition over a set period, where you also get the motivation and support from your peers going through a similar experience.

It is helpful to understand that if 11 people reduce their animal consumption by 10%, it is more than if one person is perfectly 100% vegan. Even the baby steps in the right direction are much more long-term than not doing anything. By making too many changes too quickly, our brain feels overwhelmed, protests, and takes the easiest step, falling back into old habits. Choose what feels best for you while taking part in these challenges.

VEGAN CHALLENGES

There is a good selection of challenges you could join. For example, you can sign up for Challenge22 (www.challenge22.com), where you will find guidance from dieticians and online mentors, friendly support from the network in a Facebook group, and fabulous plant-based recipes. It is a 22-day vegan experience, hence the name. For no fee and an easy sign-up form, you could be among those over 700,000 who have already joined.

Another well-known challenge is Veganuary (www.veganuary.com), where people with other new year's resolutions sign up to join the vegan lifestyle for January. In 2022 alone, over 600,000 people joined the challenge globally. All the retailers launch their new vegan products in collaboration with Veganuary, so all challenge participants and beyond benefit from a great selection of new products. Their vision is simple; they want a vegan world.

For those with less patience, there is a seven-day (www.7dayvegan.com) challenge. The goal is that in one week, you would learn more about your health, reduce your carbon footprint, and find compassion towards all other creatures.

If any of the above challenges don't inspire you, there are plenty to choose from, like Eating Well (www.eatingwell.com) or the Rainbow Plant Life (www.rainbowplantlife.com). The aim here is to commit yourself, and any of these organisations are there to keep you accountable, support you, and provide information as the process may be daunting, to begin with. Let me tell you a secret; most people find becoming vegan way easier and enjoyable once they start the journey and break preexisting stereotypes.

Hear for yourself from the people who have gone vegan by joining the challenge and sticking to it as they liked the newfound lifestyle a lot!

Challenge22 program has fixed things for me. They tell you

all the answers to questions you don't even think about asking. They have trained dieticians and one-to-one support.

✿

I joined Challenge22 and went fully vegan from day one.

✿

I did the Veganuary challenge and simply stuck to it.

✿

I was veggie for over 30 years but never liked cheese or eggs, so milk was my thing! I tried Veganuary five years ago and found oat milk as I had only ever tried soya milk before and hated it. I've never looked back.

✿

Well, I've been veggie since 10 (now 40) and started gradually removing dairy products just before Veganuary 2015. First, I switched the milk, then the butter, and cheese, and started weeding out the less obvious things with animal-derived products.

✿

I have previously shared about the great breaking point in my vegan journey. However, after further thought, everything started in my childhood. Even as a child, I consciously resisted eating animals as I always loved them. I would be watching tv series about animals and would stand for them. Even when visiting my aunty at a village, I was standing tearful with a stick in my hands and didn't let them take the calf or the horse away.

Of course, back then, I didn't know all the truth; however, still, at that young age, I managed to find out some facts and wrote "fish are friends, not food" on my pencil case. It helped that my zodiac sign was Pisces, so I had a good excuse not to eat them, saying they were my family too. In my teenage years, I avoided meat, milk, and eggs. Furthermore, as I was born in Rooster year according to the Chinse zodiac, this was yet another excuse not to consume "family members".

Naturally, I have asked my father, a semi-vegetarian, to allow me not to consume animal products. However, the response was negative, explaining that I was an athlete and required to eat.

Only when I was 21 years old did my friend share the Earthlings video with me. That was the day I altogether quit meat and, within eight months, became vegan, following Challenge22. So, to sum it up, I am doing it for animals and Earth (no one would dare litter near me). As a bonus, my health improved as I was sensitive and allergic to many substances.

I did Veganuary 2019 just to see how I got on with it without putting pressure on myself to jump straight in as a permanent change. After two weeks, I knew there would be no going back for me. I really enjoyed the guilt-free feeling of animals not suffering for my food, and as household products and toiletries ran out, I replaced them all with vegan and cruelty-free versions.

I gradually reduced my meat intake when initially going vegetarian. Later I did Veganuary to see how that would go, and bar probably the first one or two shopping trips, it went great! It took me over 25 years to crack what was causing skin issues, and while not official, it has improved dramatically since cutting out dairy. Then I looked into the ethical side, which was more than enough to decide to go vegan permanently.
Best life choice ever.

I was a full-on meat eater, and my friend talked me into doing Veganuary 2019, which I still hadn't started by the 4th of January. So, I watch Earthlings and have been vegan since the 4th of January 2019.

I became vegetarian first, then cut out eggs, dairy and honey during Veganuary 2017. Before Veganuary started, I tried out different kinds of milk in my tea until I found one I liked. I cut out cheese completely, and tried some other margarine and recipes.

I was vegetarian and had a suspected stroke at the age of 46. After lots of research, I cut out dairy too. The results were almost instant, and my health improved massively. I'm also a massive animal lover, so it made perfect sense to go vegan, and I wish I had done it years ago. Bad cholesterol is only present in meat and dairy, so cutting that out is doing your health a massive benefit for starters, let alone the ethical reasons. I also did and recommend Challenge22; they're so supportive.

I've been a strict vegetarian since I was born. My parents are veggie, and my sister and I have brought our children up vegetarian. A few years ago, my sister and niece both became vegan. I had often considered it but felt it would be difficult due to family circumstances. I also thought it would be pretty expensive, and we only have one wage to support the five of us. So anyway, one morning, I got up and decided, nope, I'm vegan, and that was me. No slip-ups, nothing, and I can honestly say I've missed nothing.

I have been vegan from birth, and it's been 47 years.

I rarely ate meat anyway, so the majority of my food was vegetarian. Thus, I just decided to ditch it all. I'm stubborn, so when I set my mind on something, I stick to it. So far, four and a half years and counting.

9 ASSOCIATION MATTERS

You imbibe your associations. Those people you closely connect with ... the conversations you have... all profoundly influence your thinking and actions. You slowly become the sum of the people closest to you. Choose them wisely.
Adela Akoo

There is a saying – "Show me your friends, I'll show you your future"- that the people you surround yourself with are your reflection. Therefore, if you have a group of vegan friends, you will likely inevitably pick up some habits, be it for shopping for household items or eating. It is usually unintentional, but through communication and simply being who you are, people prefer to associate and act similarly. It is especially true for family members since they usually spend more time together.

In a way, I could say that my story of how I became vegan is through association with the right people. Years before, I have seen a few documentaries about animal farming and the cruel industry, not only for the non-human animals involved but also for humans through antimicrobial resistance, infective disease, and risk for the pandemics. It was about ten years ago, while I studied Biomedical Science, hence the latter topic was particularly interesting. I am writing this book during the COVID-19 pandemic. In general, the pandemic was not a question of if but when, and we've all felt its consequences.

Shamefully I made no change in my lifestyle, even though I was deeply disturbed by the documentaries I watched years ago and continue carrying mental images to this day. Perhaps I reduced the meat for a week and talked to one of my friends about considering being vegetarian. Being in the social bubble that was nothing like vegans or vegetarians, I, unfortunately, continued with my comfortable old habits. However, the change happened when I met a few people who were plant-based and were able to share their experiences, motives, and their vegan stories with me. It got me curious and led to some reading, particularly about health aspects and how being an "animal lover" is hypocritical if you are having one of them for dinner. Listening to a TED talk on speciesism was what ultimately influenced me the most. Yet not as much as having the right people around me that can show that being vegan is not only possible but relatively straightforward and rewarding. Learning from someone you trust and have a relationship with is much more powerful and encourages you to take action since the credibility factor is also at play.

The following stories will give you an insight into how much influence someone can have in the lives of other people, sometimes without evening knowing it.

I have been vegetarian for about twelve years and became vegan, encouraged by my boyfriend. I participated in a challenge to eat plant-based foods and exercise for a month. It felt great on my body. Also, in the meantime, I was educating myself further on veganism, and here we are, that one month is still lasting.

I have a vegan friend who influenced me to choose the right path, first by suggesting to watch Earthlings. I always loved animals but never thought how hypocritical it was to love them and eat them simultaneously. The documentary changed my understanding of many things. I wasn't able to finish watching it and cried a lot. Thinking I would never be able to cut off cheese and other products, I have become vegetarian. Nevertheless, I learned about the cruelty in the dairy and egg industries and decided to stop pouring all that nonsense into my body. I became vegan and couldn't believe how much easier it was than the preconceived idea.

I was vegetarian until I met a nice vegan girl. Her energetic state really impressed me. After that, I became more interested in veganism until I tried it and couldn't be happier and more energetic.

We followed suit after our 16-year-old daughter became vegan. We have loved getting ideas and inspiration from Max La Manna, Miguel Barclay, The Happy Pear, and many other vegan social media foodies. We love using up whatever needs eating and inventing recipes now. Veganism is on the rise, so things can only get even better.

My daughter and son-in-law were living the vegan lifestyle. So, after conversing with them about the meat industry horrors and tasting some of their vegan dishes, I took the step! Best decision I've made in years!

My daughter has educated me. She showed me lots of videos, and we discussed and made some vegan food. After eating plant-based meals, I felt really good; I didn't have that heavy feeling in my stomach.

The example of my friend influenced my decision to go vegan. I have challenged myself to see how my well-being will change. Later, once I educated myself, I found other reasons to stay vegan.

My son became vegan four years ago. He nagged me for a year to change. Finally, I gave in and said I would do it for a month to please and shut him up. After the month, I felt so much better I never looked back. I've just had my third vegan anniversary.

I've read a book by Sri Sathya Sai Baba, where it is written that you will never elevate one step above as long as you are eating meat. The one who consumes meat receives animal properties and suffering. Eating meat is a sin; eating fish is a mistake.

I thought about it and became vegan in a minute. Gradually my family joined me too.

I went vegan three years ago after watching the documentary Dairy is Scary. Hubby thought I was mad. Yet, in less than three months, he was vegan as well. My only regret is I didn't do it sooner.

I was in the punk/hardcore scene in the 90s, and vegan and animal rights were a big thing. It was easy to be vegan in that scene. Twenty-six years later, my favourite band is still the most righteous human rights and animal liberation supporting band.

It seems daunting at first to check labels, etc., but it soon becomes second nature. My husband went vegetarian with me but said going vegan would take it too far. I came home from work almost three years ago to find out my husband had been talking to our vegan daughter on the phone for over an hour and decided we would give it a go. She was so happy she cried. Now he says it's one of the best things he's ever done, and he's 66 years old, and we both agree we are vegan for life.

My veganism journey started by reading books on healthy living and associating with people who already lead a healthy vegan lifestyle.

10 NEVER SAY NEVER

Change will not come if we wait for some other person or some other time. We are the ones we've been waiting for. We are the change that we seek.
Barack Obama

The final chapter is intended for those who have not yet committed to veganism but have contemplated making this change.

Perhaps you are sceptical, mocking others for being vegan or offering snidey comments if a colleague or family member offers a vegan cake or burger. Maybe you refuse to eat the beautiful lasagna your daughter-in-law made simply because it's vegan. You look at vegan food with prejudice that it is bland and unsatisfying. Bear with me because the most hardcore carnivores who previously swore never to become vegetarians, let alone vegans, are now enjoying the lavish lifestyle that being vegan brings you. The future holds many opportunities to change for the better, and this may be your sign to take a step.

I have to admit; I was one of those people who said I could never be vegan. I loved eating eggs too much and thought I couldn't live without cottage cheese. I could only imagine barbeques with the pork, and Christmas eve without a herring seemed a mission impossible. However, as time passes, you learn new things, associate with new people, and realise that some food items are worth so much less than peace within yourself and knowing that your eating habits are not the reason someone miserably lost their life. Also, my mum is the most fantastic cook, which made it more challenging to switch, but I am so grateful that she is open to cooking some delicious vegan dishes and always up for a challenge to experiment with new recipes.

If reading this book has inspired you to go vegan, I would love to hear from you, and so that others benefit too, please share your vegan story on any social media with a #MyVeganStory. To finish on a hopeful note, here are the stories from vegans who swore they could never go vegan.

September 2020, I said, "I could never be vegan". I was trialling two weeks plant-based in support of my daughter with her medical needs. Well, let me tell you, I have never looked back, and now I am very loud and proud to be vegan.

I used to say I could never be vegan. But I have learned to never say never about many things.

One day a switch flipped, and I never looked back. But, like most vegans, I wish I had only done it sooner.

I used to think, "it's so hard to be vegan and be healthy". But I have read books, watched the reality of the animal industry, and stopped there and then. It's a level of consciousness.

I remember thinking that I could never go vegan, and now I run a website called vegan nutrition and tips. But I could never go back!

I typically ate a whole packet of bacon in a sandwich and regularly ate a 1 kg bag of nuggets in an evening. I couldn't picture being vegan, but it was straightforward once I started. As a result, I eat far better, lost weight, have more energy, and feel less guilty.

I used to say that as well, and now I don't see myself ever ditching my plant-based diet. It feels too good being vegan to go back eating animal products.

I remember saying that to my friend who was in transitioning vegan phase a few years back. Little did I know I would turn into one as well. Now I just wonder why haven't I been vegan far longer.

I was a total anti-vegan! I went vegan after watching What the Health five years ago. It is hands down the best decision I have ever made. I went from being pre-diabetic with arthritis to astounding my doctor last year with my excellent blood panel.

I remember my friend saying she had given up sausages for health. I thought to myself that I could never do that. PS: there are some fabulous vegan sausages out there! So technically, I was right in that I could never give up sausages.

I never thought I could commit to being vegan until I stopped repeating that thought and started thinking more about what I could do. I became vegan seven years ago when I was 56 years old.

ABOUT THE AUTHOR

Raminta has been vegan for over three years, and during that time, the passion for veganism only grew stronger. She is deeply intrigued by why people struggle to relate to vegans since, deep down, we all want to be kind. The stories of individual veganism journeys inspired Raminta. Being a scientist, she wanted to learn more about why and how people become vegan and thus collected, studied and organised unique stories for others to enjoy, get enthused and motivated to lead a lifestyle full of kindness and compassion towards animals and people alike.

Raminta lives in Cambridgeshire, UK, with a soon-to-be husband, Tomas, and shares their home with a cat named Mango.

If you have made it this far in the book and have enjoyed it, please leave a review. I would love to hear your thoughts!

If you would like to be part of a positive, vegan community, follow me on Twitter @YourVeganStory

BIBLIOGRAPHY

[1]   N.-G. Wunsch, "Veganuary - statistics and facts," *https://www.statista.com/topics/8918/veganuary/#topicHeader__wrapper*, Mar. 2022.

[2]   Veganuary, "VEGANUARY 2022 IS OFFICIALLY THE BIGGEST YEAR YET – AND STILL RISING," *https://veganuary.com/veganuary-2022-biggest-year-yet/#:~:text=18th%20January%202022%20%E2%80%94%20Veganuary%2C%20a,year's%20total%20of%20580%2C000%20participants.*, Jan. 2022.

[3]   S. KARTIK and Happy Cow, "The Growth of Vegan Restaurants in Europe, 2022," *https://www.happycow.net/blog/the-growth-of-vegan-restaurants-in-europe-2022/*, May 2022.

[4]   L. Marino, "Thinking chickens: a review of cognition, emotion, and behaviour in the domestic chicken," *Animal Cognition*, vol. 20, no. 2, pp. 127–147, 2017.

[5]   R. Rugani, G. Vallortigara, K. Priftis, and L. Regolin, "Number-space mapping in the newborn chick resembles humans' mental number line," *Science (1979)*, vol. 347, no. 6221, pp. 534–536, 2015.

[6]   S. M. Abeyesinghe, C. J. Nicol, S. J. Hartnell, and C. M. Wathes, "Can domestic fowl, Gallus gallus domesticus, show self-control?," *Animal Behaviour*, vol. 70, no. 1, pp. 1–11, 2005.

[7]   W. Mischel, E. B. Ebbesen, and A. Raskoff Zeiss, "Cognitive and attentional mechanisms in delay of gratification.," *J Pers Soc Psychol*, vol. 21, no. 2, p. 204, 1972.

[8]   L. Marino and C. M. Colvin, "Thinking pigs," *International Journal of Comparative Psychology*, vol. 28, 2015.

[9]   L. Marino and K. Allen, "The Psychology of Cows," *Animal Behavior and Cognition*, vol. 4, no. 4, pp. 474–498, Nov. 2017, DOI: 10.26451/abc.04.04.06.2017.

[10] The Humane League, "DAIRY COWS: HOW LONG DO DAIRY CATTLE LIVE? DO THEY SUFFER?," https://thehumaneleague.org/article/dairy-cows, August 2022.

[11] M. Coulon, C. Baudoin, Y. Heyman, and B. L. Deputte, "Cattle discriminate between familiar and unfamiliar conspecifics by using only head visual cues," *Animal Cognition*, vol. 14, no. 2, pp. 279–290, 2011.

[12] L. Marino and D. Merskin, "Intelligence, complexity, and individuality in sheep," *Animal Sentience*, vol. 4, no. 25, Jan. 2019, DOI: 10.51291/2377-7478.1374.

[13] L. Greiveldinger, I. Veissier, and A. Boissy, "The ability of lambs to form expectations and the emotional consequences of a discrepancy from their expectations," *Psychoneuroendocrinology*, vol. 36, no. 6, pp. 806–815, 2011.

[14] M. Springmann, H. C. J. Godfray, M. Rayner, and P. Scarborough, "Analysis and valuation of the health and climate change cobenefits of dietary change," *Proceedings of the National Academy of Sciences*, vol. 113, no. 15, pp. 4146–4151, 2016.

[15] N. Wright, L. Wilson, M. Smith, B. Duncan, and P. McHugh, "The BROAD study: A randomized controlled trial using a whole food plant-based diet in the community for obesity, ischaemic heart disease or diabetes," *Nutr Diabetes*, vol. 7, no. 3, pp. e256–e256, 2017.

[16] Z. H. Gan, H. C. Cheong, Y.-K. Tu, and P.-H. Kuo, "Association between plant-based dietary patterns and risk of cardiovascular disease: a systematic review and meta-analysis of prospective cohort studies," *Nutrients*, vol. 13, no. 11, p. 3952, 2021.

[17] H. Kim *et al.*, "Plant-based diets, pescatarian diets and COVID-19 severity: a population-based case-control study in six countries," *BMJ Nutrition, Prevention & Health*, vol. 4, no. 1, p. 257, 2021.

[18]   J. Merino *et al.*, "Diet quality and risk and severity of COVID-19: a prospective cohort study," *Gut,* vol. 70, no. 11, pp. 2096–2104, 2021.

[19]   M. A. Storz, "Lifestyle Adjustments in Long-COVID Management: Potential Benefits of Plant-Based Diets. Current Nutrition Reports, 10 (4), 352–363." 2021.

Printed in Poland
by Amazon Fulfillment
Poland Sp. z o.o., Wrocław

94632142R00060